Soon She Will Be Dead

SOON

SHE WILL BE

DEAD

a comprehensive guide to losing your parent
without losing your mind

BRITA LONG

SOON SHE WILL BE DEAD
*A Comprehensive Guide to Losing Your
Parent Without Losing Your Mind*

ISBN   978-1-5445-0389-9 *Hardcover*
      978-1-5445-0387-5 *Paperback*
      978-1-5445-0388-2 *Ebook*

For Beatrice Long and Michael Johnson

CONTENTS

INTRODUCTION..9

1. GETTING REAL 15

2. PRACTICAL STEPS TO SURVIVE THE EMOTIONS
   AROUND YOUR PARENTS AGING AND DYING..33

3. THE TOXIC PARENT 61

4. WHAT YOU CAN EXPECT...................................69

5. TIME MANAGEMENT, ACTUALLY
   SELF-MANAGEMENT 97

6. SELF-CARE 119

7. ELDER ABUSE...141

8. OTHERS...153

9. MONEY 167

10. ESTATE PLANNING..185

11. AFTER DEATH..205

CONCLUSION..217

ABOUT BRITA LONG...221

INTRODUCTION

"I'm glad my mother is dead."

That was the thought that went through my head when my mother died.

I am an attorney and have been for over two decades. I have been a deputy prosecuting attorney, family law attorney, and estate law attorney. I love the law and got into it because it is interesting, I enjoy it and, I know it upside down, left, right, and center. I know revocable living trusts like the back of my hand. You don't know what that is and don't need to know what that is. That is my job to know. That is why you pay me to set up your estate plan. I thought I knew what I needed to know to do my job well, and I did a good job and helped a lot of people.

However, when my mom became ill and died, my entire

world was turned upside down because I realized I didn't know anything. I thought my job as an attorney was to get the legal stuff right, but when my mom died, I learned that the legal stuff is a tiny fraction, an important fraction—in fact, crucial—but it is a tiny fraction of what you have to get right to navigate a parent's death.

What I didn't realize was how important the financial aspects would be, how important the social aspects would be, how important self-care would be, and how others would react. Do you ever think you need to be told to drink water, eat, or sleep? No, of course not—until you are sitting next to your dad's hospital bed and you don't know when he is going to die, and you are afraid to leave because you don't want that to be the last time you have seen him. And if you don't leave you feel like you are going to die of exhaustion. What do you do then? I didn't know.

This book is meant to fill in the gaps, so you can understand not just what to do legally (and, make no mistake, you must get that one correct), but also all of the other things so that, when the inevitable happens, and your mom or dad goes, you are prepared to handle that the best possible way and get through to the other side.

Mine is the same journey and pain that you are likely to go through. No one tells you how to get through "this."

While people may ask how you are doing, most really don't want to know. Before you get a word out, they have moved on, and your only socially acceptable answer is, "Oh, I'm fine."

No one talks about the work, exhaustion, difficulty in making decisions, grief, frustration, or hard feelings of taking care of one's aging or ill parents, much less how to make things better. And most certainly no one talks about the relief one feels when your parent dies or the following guilt about feeling said relief.

By reading this book, you will know that you are not alone, you're not going crazy, you are not a horrible person, you will not die yourself from this process, and, if done properly, you will come through this experience with some bruises and scrapes but with your head still attached.

In this book, you will learn about all of the issues that you will need to navigate when you move into the role of caretaker for one or both of your parents, what your duties should and will be, and how to carry those out ethically, efficiently, and with compassion. Everything from finances, to family relationships, to social relationships, to your own kids, to the legal issues involved, to how to deal with your own emotions and other people's emotions. Everything from soup to nuts is in this book.

Other lawyers can help you with estate and money planning at the end of your parent's life. Some of them might even do a better job than me. But I can help you with the self-care, relationship issues, emotional troubles, and, yes, even the estate planning, because I've lived this shit—not once, but twice.

This book is not for the lazy. It is not a feel-good, fix-your-childhood-issues, sing-kumbaya, or get-rich-quick book. You are going to have to put your big-kid pants on, do some soul searching, do some hard work, and sit with some very uncomfortable feelings. For you who are willing to do this work, there is great reward. You will be the exception. You will get through this process without losing your shit.

Although this book is written from a female perspective, both men and women will benefit from reading it. If your parent has a protracted illness, the entirety of this book will be beneficial. However, even if your parent's death is sudden, you will still find information that will soften the blow of losing your parent.

Specific names have been altered to protect the privacy and confidentiality of clients throughout the book.

The train is leaving whether you're on it or not. Are you ready to get on it and prepare yourself for this journey and maybe actually come out of it better than you went in? If so, then let's go.

Chapter One

GETTING REAL

━━━

*The moment you accept what troubles
you've been given, the door will open.*

—RUMI

To lie to others is to be dishonest. To lie to oneself is to commit suicide. I have been an attorney for a long time and have seen many people go to great lengths to deny the obvious. I have never seen anyone's life benefit from this. It might feel better at the time and appear to be "easier" to just ignore the headlights that are headed straight for you, but it will kill you in the end.

I, too, have a well-honed habit of lying to myself and telling myself it is "fine." I have learned that habit so that I don't have anxiety attacks that could land me in real trouble. I have vacillated between terror, totally being paralyzed, and ignoring the issue right up until the last minute, when I know I need to act to prevent a total catastrophe.

For those of us who have anxiety issues, walking this fine line is tricky, and we get it wrong a lot. However, I keep working so that I am gradually moving toward the center of the two extremes.

Your first step, in keeping your shit together when your parent is aging or dying, is to find your honesty center. This is happening. One day you are going to wake up and not have a mom, or a dad, or you will be an orphan.

And I don't mean in some nebulous, hard-to-think-about fifteen to thirty years from now. I mean like maybe last Christmas was your last Christmas with him or her. For some of you, this is going to be the first time someone close to you has died. I do not envy you. You may think you have felt pain, but friend, you have not.

I am slapping you across the face so that you can't go into denial. Yes, it is "easier" and feels better to think, "Well, my mom has the best doctors around, and she will be fine." And this thinking is going to cause you to throw away the absolute most precious resource you have: time. Especially time with your mom. Even if your mom or dad makes a miraculous recovery, that just means a delay, not a cancellation. Whether "this" happens next week, next year, or in ten years, it is going to happen. There is no harm in being somewhat prepared, and there is a disaster waiting if you aren't.

My dad had twice come about as close to dying as one can without actually dying—one year apart, almost to the day. The first time I was totally unprepared. Even though my job was to deal with preparing for death and dealing with the aftermath, I was a mess when I arrived at the ICU and saw my stronger-than-the-Marlboro-man dad unconscious with 101 tubes in every square inch of his body, including a ventilator.

True to my father's style, he was back working on the construction site three months later, carrying his oxygen tank with him. The next January I was again boarding an emergency flight to Billings, Montana, where he was in the same ICU with the same issues. This time I didn't fall apart. I knew the drill.

For that year, I had also treated every day he was around as a gift.

Once again, within a few weeks, my father was out of the hospital. This time he was a little worse for wear, though. Then, nearly one more year later, my father did actually die, in the middle of me writing this book. I am not kidding. It is still difficult at times to actually accept that my father is dead. However, wishing doesn't make it so.

In addition to your own denial, you must also recognize that it is probably really difficult for your parent to accept that he or she is actually dying as well. You are losing a parent. Your parent is losing his or her life. I heard a Southern quote that I love: "Everybody wants to go to heaven, but no one wants to die to get there."

My mother was eighty-one when she died. She had fought cancer before. Her father, mother, and sister all died of cancer. She was eighty years old and it was back with a vengeance. She had been in assisted living care and even moved over to the "more care" side of the building. It was clear to everyone that my mom was not going to rebound from this one. Anyone but my mother, that is—and she had been a nurse.

I remember when her oncologist gently and kindly told her that he thought it was probably time to call in hospice. In my thirty-two years I had never seen such a shocked look on my mother's face. Then I caught my own facial expression, which was a "Huh, what did you think he was going to say, Mom? Are you kidding me? Of course, it is time to call hospice." I was so surprised that she was shocked. I don't think my mom noticed my face, and I pray to God she didn't. I could have handled it with a tad more kindness and compassion. I have never been told I was dying, so I have no idea what that feels like, but I imagine denial is the first emotion.

It is totally natural to have denial at the beginning of this process. It is also important for you to move past that denial fairly quickly. If you don't acknowledge the reality of the situation, you can't prepare for it. I will share two stories about denial, of two women in similar situations with very different outcomes.

One woman was my friend Nicki. She was in her early thirties, a high-powered bigwig at Microsoft, married, and had two children—one under six months old. She was in good shape and had a very healthy lifestyle. In the late summer, she hit her leg on a table and the bruise refused to heal. She went to her doctor and, in a whirlwind of a few days, had been diagnosed with stage 4 lymphoma. She was given less than a year to live.

It would have been incredibly easy for her to go into denial and stay there. Of all of the people to receive a death sentence—her? She was an amazing person. She had so much love to give and received so much love from incredible people and had a solid support system. She had unlimited resources and could, and did, get the best medical care in the world. She was young, healthy, and had two babies to care for. Are you fucking kidding me?

Yet she didn't go into denial. She didn't feel sorry for herself. She took a few weeks to think, absorb, and comfort herself, and then she started taking care of business. She had me take lots of photographs of her and the kids. She made videos for the kids of her doing tasks she wanted to teach them but wouldn't be able to, such as how to put on makeup, make a bed, and so on, as well as life lessons she wanted to teach them. She bought gifts for the kids to be opened at important times during their lives. Her estate plan was in proper order. She planned a trip to Hawaii for her entire family. That trip didn't happen, but she tried.

That Christmas she invited my son and me to Christmas dinner. I couldn't believe her generosity. She and everyone else knew this would be her last Christmas, yet she invited us to join them. I will never forget that Christmas. No one was in denial about what was happening. Bill and Melinda Gates sent over a case of great wine. We ate, laughed, played games, napped on the couch holding babies, and took pictures.

That next spring, her goal was to make it to her son's first birthday, and she did. She had done everything she could possibly do to ease this transition for her children, herself, and her family. She died that spring in her own bed, surrounded by her family. When I talked with her husband a week later, the way he described it was nothing short of beautiful.

I will never forget Nicki or the gifts that she gave me, much less the gifts that she gave to her family, especially her children. Imagine losing your mother shortly after you turned one. You would have no memory of her at all. Yet Nicki's son not only has the stories told by other people and photographs, he also has videos for him from his mother. He has letters specifically to him from his mother. When he approaches important events in his life, he knows that his mother will be there and that he will receive an actual gift from her. He isn't just told by others that he was loved and treasured; he is shown that directly by his mother, on a continual basis. None of that could have been possible if she had denied what was really happening.

The cost of denial is wasted time and wasted opportunity. The other side of the coin was my client Pam, who was literally days, if not hours, away from death when we met. I had been called to talk to her and then prepare her estate plan. After learning of her health reality, I rushed to her hospital bed, talked with her for a few hours, then rushed back to the office. Our office was able to complete a revocable living trust and other documents within thirty hours. This fast turnaround time is fairly unheard of. We then rushed back to the hospital and were able to get her signature on the documents and trust funded before she passed. We got it all done, although that is not how I like to work and it was very stressful for all concerned. Had her family happened to call another attorney, I am confident the outcome would not have been so successful.

Pam had been told her fate over six months prior to calling me. She had three adult children, but still young, one of whom was an active drug addict, and nearly $3 million in her estate. Had I not been able to do the work I did, her drug-addicted daughter would have been given a check for at least $850,000. One can imagine what would have happened when she got that money.

When talking with Pam, she had such relief that she had properly protected her children, even if just from themselves. She mentioned that she had "tried" to do "this" online herself a few months prior. I am so thankful that she had not been able to complete whatever online crap she had tried. It would have been a total disaster, yet she would have thought she had done the right thing.

Why did it take her and her family so long to call me after she knew her fate? I don't know and I wasn't about to question her about it. The only answer I can come up with is that it took her that long and being that sick in the hospital to really absorb and acknowledge that she was about to die. She had not prepared herself or her family for her death. We were able to save her kids from what would have been a second disaster—on top of losing their mom. However, her financial accounts were still not in order; her home was not in order; and her relationships were not in order. Although the mess was smaller, she still left her family a mess, not a legacy.

I am not judging her. I have never been told that I only have a short time to live. I hope that I would be willing to acknowledge the truth, after my short pity party, to do what I needed to do to protect my family and prepare them as much as I could for a life without me. That only happens if you are not in denial.

So yes, this is happening. Acknowledge it truly and to be kind to yourself and be kind to the person who is actually dying. Other than your perception that it will save you pain (it won't, really), there is absolutely no benefit of denying the truth about what is happening.

What about hope, you ask? Isn't acknowledging what is happening giving up hope? Absolutely not. I am a very positive and hopeful person. Without hope, I would have given up decades ago. It is vital both to have hope and to do what you can do in the meantime. If I am on the road and I see a train coming at me, yes, I hope that I can get off the tracks before the train hits me. At the same time, I also use my legs to get the heck off the railroad tracks.

I lived in the Pacific Northwest for twenty-one years. In Seattle, I lived on top of a hill. I hoped that I would never experience a major earthquake, much less one followed by a tsunami. That didn't stop me from having a solid earthquake kit along with a huge barrel of clean water at all times.

Every day, one hopes that one doesn't get in a car accident *and* one wears their seatbelt and (hopefully) doesn't look at their phone. So, hope and prepare.

IT IS GOING TO SUCK

I have a mother and a father. However, they had never met. My father was nineteen when I was born. He was never contacted when I was born or given an opportunity to have any say in my life, much less be in my life. I was in three different foster homes until I was adopted at six months old.

My mother adopted me when she was a forty-eight-year-old single mother. We lived with my grandmother, who died when I was three. Given my mother's age, and living with my grandmother, I grew up around older people. I experienced far more death than any other child I knew: my grandma, a close aunt, a close cousin, a childhood friend, and others. I thought I knew the level of pain I would experience when losing my mom.

No, I didn't.

I am not a psychologist. I do have some common sense, though. The only reason you are alive is due to your parents. Not only did they bring you into the world, one or both of them (or whoever else cared for you) literally kept you alive for many years. Your entire existence and whether you lived or died was 100 percent dependent on this one or maybe two people.

I don't care how old you are; there is something completely visceral about the threat of losing that one person. If that person dies, how are you going to stay alive? No, it doesn't make logical sense. You are an adult, you are financially independent, and you are not going to die when your parent dies. But the cells in your body don't know that.

I have not lost a child. Thank God. Other than that pain, I really can't think of pain that would be greater than losing one's parent. It sucks. It goes into places in your body that you didn't know you had. Know that it is going to be horrible, and know that it will get better and one day, as Joe Biden says, "you will smile when you think of them instead of cry."

Again, rationality doesn't have much to do with this topic. You may think "this isn't fair," even though you are an adult and know that life is not fair; that doesn't matter.

Absent some extreme circumstance, you are never going to be ready to lose your parent. I found my father when I was twenty-three years old. My father and I were extremely close. We talked at least once a day and would have talked probably five times a day if he had his way. We both missed out on a lot in those twenty-three years. My relationship with my father is one of the greatest gifts I have ever received in my life. I was not ready to let it go.

During our final meeting of doctors, social workers, nurses, and chaplains when my father was dying, I remember crying out that "I'm not ready." The social worker came over, held me, and told me that I would never be ready; no one is ever "ready."

FEAR

When you start to get scared or have anxiety, it is helpful to take a few seconds or minutes to really examine what you are scared of. Is that fear a true likelihood? If so, what is the worst that is going to happen? Can you live through that? For instance, when my mom was dying, I feared so many things. I had a new law practice that was still struggling; I was a single parent with a son who was coming out, acting out, and losing his grandma. I was in a loving but unhealthy relationship with my now ex-husband, who was an alcoholic. Life was a fucking mess. I had legitimate things to be concerned about. Could I keep a struggling law practice afloat when I couldn't work more than twenty-five hours a week? When would the next call come about my son getting into major trouble? And how long was I going to have to live like this? How long can one live in total survival mode?

Early on, I made a conscious decision that I would do what needed to be done for my mom, even if it meant losing my business. Even if it meant I would have to wait tables again and start over, then so be it. That never happened, but it freed me from having to struggle with difficult decisions every day about how to spend my time and funds.

One of the difficult things about the experience of watching your parent die is that you have no idea when it will end. I can and have accomplished much in my life. I have run marathons. I can do just about anything if I know what I am supposed to do and how long it is going to take. Tell me to run 26.2 miles and, with some training, I can do it. But don't tell me to run 15 miles and then, toward the end, tell me to run another 11.2.

Law school—no problem. It is just three years, and I can do it. Bar exam—six hours a day to study for a few months and then three days of hell and done. Hell, even childbirth has a fairly firm end time. No one is in labor for a week.

Well, that is not how this process works. Believe me, I tried every conceivable way to get someone with any authority to give me some time frame, plan, anything so that I could cope. There isn't one.

This reality makes planning one's life, especially if one is a planner, rather difficult. Can I go to that meeting in a month? I don't know. How long do I need to worry about not bringing in money? I don't know. How long can I keep my job, since when I am there I am not focused? I don't know. How long do I have to arrange doctors' visits, transportation visits, and sleeping at the assisted living facility in a chair? I don't know. When will I have time to be able to get my brows waxed again? I don't know. How long will I be in absolute survival mode? I don't know. Just keep hanging on.

For planners, this can be excruciatingly painful. All structure is tossed out the door. All order is tossed with it. You don't know if you are coming or going, and you don't know how long this is going to last. Most of the time, you don't know what end is up—so how can you dig your way out of this?

You are just going to have to deal with it. It will be helpful to follow the advice later on in the book about time and self-management. It will also help to not look at the big picture, but only take small bites. Don't look at the entire huge staircase in front of you—just the one stair you need to get to next. One stair at a time.

Years ago, I climbed Mount Rainier. We had gotten past the clouds and had been on snow for a while. I could see

Camp Muir in the distance. Thank God. I was so tired, and every step was an effort. We kept putting one foot in front of the other. Over an hour went by and I looked up, and the building had not moved. It was not any bigger. I swear I had been walking on a treadmill. It was so disheartening, I nearly cried.

This situation is your own walk in the snow. You are not even going to be able to see a light at the end of the tunnel, Camp Muir, or whatever other analogy you want to insert. Just know it is there, and you will get to it. You really are making progress, even if you can't see it.

One of the reasons this book is so important is that if you are a caregiver, you are more likely to die faster than the one you are caring for. True fact. Caretakers are so overwhelmed, so stressed out, and emotionally fraught that they age faster and get sicker than the people they are caring for. We will get to self-care later on, but know that if you do things properly, you will get to the other side of this thing with a few scratches but no threatening injuries.

If you have ever had any financial difficulty, you know that feeling in the pit of your stomach when you see a bill in the mailbox or inbox. It is horrible. You see the envelope and immediately know what it is. You also immediately know that you don't have the money to pay the bill. You may or may not have a bit of cushion until the due date, but regardless, you can't pay it. You feel shame. You are embarrassed. You may be defensive and think about why "this" isn't your fault. At the same time, you know that the person or company at the other end of that bill could care less. They just want, and have a right to, their money. This feeling lasts. It doesn't go away.

So, what do most people do? Don't open the bill. It sits quietly on the counter, but it isn't quiet, is it? It whispers to you every time you pass by: "I'm still here and you are still a loser who can't pay me." You keep ignoring it, and the pile and the chorus of bills grows. Now you have two bills from the electric company. Those voices are really getting loud.

The only way to shut the voices up is to just deal with them. Open the damn bills. Many times, the bills are lower than you thought they would be. Maybe you can pay half of that bill and at least buy yourself another month. Maybe you can pick up an extra shift and pay off that bill entirely. But nothing good comes from not opening the bills.

So now is the time to get your big-girl or big-boy pants on and face what needs to be faced. Commit to doing what needs to be done. The good news is that just by reading this book you have come a long way, so congratulate yourself for stepping up. You are ahead of the curve and the exception. You are not going to live in denial. You will understand reality and thus can clearly plan, as much as one can, for the future. You can prioritize what is really important to do with your time and how you can help care for your parent. You are being honest with yourself. You are not telling yourself lies that will only get you in trouble.

Chapter Two

PRACTICAL STEPS TO SURVIVE THE EMOTIONS AROUND YOUR PARENTS AGING AND DYING

It is not the strongest or the most intelligent who will survive, but those who can best manage change.
—LEON MEGGINSON

Change is a coming, friend. The wind is beginning to shift, and soon you will be in a pretty good storm. Best to begin adjusting your sails.

Every situation is different. Every family is different, and every person reading this is different and has different responsibilities. Some will be able to take time off of work. Some will not. Some will have lots of support from others, and many will have to go it alone. Some have their own kids to care for, and others don't. However, we all have responsibilities and a life that needs our attention. Whether your mom is dying or not, your five-year-old still needs a bath tonight.

What everyone does have in common is that, sooner or later during this process, you are going to have to go into survival mode. Knowing that is coming your way and being prepared for it, as much as one can, will make all of the difference in the condition you are in when you emerge from this experience.

Human beings are incredibly resilient. Many people seem indestructible and can survive nearly anything. I think of Senator John McCain and his fellow airmen surviving prison camps or the individuals who have survived concentration camps. The women who have lived through horrible conflicts in which they were systematically raped, over and over again, as a tool of war.

This event is nothing compared to what other people have lived through. You can totally get through this rather unscathed, but only if you adjust your thinking and behaviors quickly. Depending on your parent's condition, you may have time to plan and adjust your life and behaviors. Or you could be on a plane, rushing to the ICU with only a few hours to rethink your routine, responsibilities, and how life will be now. The faster you get into survival mode, the more prepared you will be. Remember, you don't know how long this experience is going to last. You are setting out for a journey and you don't know when it will end.

It may help to think of it like this. You are not preparing for a hike that you know will only last a day or two. You are preparing for a hike that could last a day, two months, or two years. So how would you prepare and pack for such a hike? You wouldn't try to take enough food and water for two years, would you? You couldn't carry all of that with you. You would take the bare minimum you would need to survive: a quality tent, sleeping bag, compass, beacon, good shoes and socks, a water filter, knowledge and tools so that you could find and eat food, a map, and as much food and water as you could comfortably carry.

Is that hike going to be comfortable if it lasts more than a few days after your food runs out? Probably not, but you will be able to survive it. That is what we are striving for here. Having the tools you will need to survive, regardless of the length of this trip.

WHAT ARE THE BARE BASICS YOU NEED TO SURVIVE?

As I write this, I am curled up in bed covered with blankets and a feather duvet. It is a cold Texas day (yes, it does get to freezing and below in Texas), and my heat is out. It is fifty-six degrees in the house and will only get colder. Nothing, and I mean nothing, matters right now other than me getting warm and then staying warm. The repairman will be here in three hours. All of my other needs are met, and my safety, much less life, is not in any real danger. That fact doesn't matter. *All* that matters to me right now is getting warm.

When your most basic needs are not being met, nothing else matters. You can't concentrate on anything else. You really could not care less about anything else. Thankfully, most of us have never been, nor ever will be, in a situation where our most basic needs are not being met.

When one is facing a very stressful and taxing situation, such as caring for another adult, it is surprising how quickly we can forget to meet our most basic needs.

So, what are the absolute minimum things we need in order to be able to survive? You need a safe and climate-appropriate place to live, clean water, food with some nutrients, regular bathing (hopefully daily), basic grooming and clean teeth, sufficient sleep, some cash flow to meet the above needs, and to take care of or arrange for someone else to take care of the bare basic responsibilities for people who are dependent on you—like your kids. Also, if you have physical or mental health issues, it is critical to take your medication. Nothing is going to get you off the rails faster, as you well know, than not taking your meds.

This is really all you need to survive. You may not look so pretty when you haven't groomed properly in a week, but you can live. Remember this when you are waking up in a chair in a hospital room. Seriously, if you are clean, watered, and fed, got a little sleep, and have twenty dollars in your pocket, you are okay.

Why am I writing about something so elementary? We are highly functional adults who know how to take a bath, so thanks anyway. You would be surprised just how easy it is when you are this stressed, anxious, taxed, and maybe in a depressed state to "forget" to eat. To try to get away with four hours of sleep a night. To not drink sufficient water and get dehydrated. To realize at 9:30 p.m. that you didn't shower that day. To be so exhausted that you justify not brushing your teeth before you go to bed.

I call out a special warning to those with mental health issues, especially depression or anxiety. If you have ever had depression, you know just how easy it can be to sit and watch TV for hour after hour and not shower that day. When you have an anxiety attack you are paralyzed; it can last for hours, a full day, or more. Nothing gets done. Nothing matters. You are going to have to be extra diligent about taking care of your mental health during this time. You cannot get away with not taking your meds— even for a day. You cannot get away with not seeing your mental health provider as directed. If your mental health deteriorates, even a little, the whole thing falls apart.

Part of taking care of our survival needs is making sure you don't run out of anything you will really need. "Well that won't happen to me; I am a highly functional adult." You will be surprised how easy it is to go to take your medication and find one pill left in the bottle. Go to feed the dog and find you only have one serving of kibble, and that is three-quarters of normal. The last thing you need is to go to pay for dinner and have your debit card rejected because you forgot to deposit that check or transfer funds. You probably can just pay the bill with another card. And the incident is still embarrassing and very stressful. Yes, all of those things are easily fixed *and* you don't need that additional stress or scrambling to add an emergency dog-food run to your day.

I had a friend, Ellie, who, on paper, had her act together. She was a successful professional, her husband had a good job, they had a small child, and they owned a nice home. During one particularly stressful period of her life, basic things began to fall apart. At her son's birthday party, her husband had to run to the store to buy toilet paper. Another time, I watched their young son in the evening and gave him a bath. I wasn't sure what to do when I found that there was not one clean towel in the house. Not even a clean hand towel. So, what did I do? I grabbed a hair dryer and dried him off. He thought it was fun, and we managed to get the job done.

So, as elementary as it sounds, it is vital that you ensure that your most basic survival needs are being met every single day. If you need to set an alarm to eat, then do that. If you need to rent a hotel room to get a good night's sleep once a week, then do that. Seriously. Your most basic needs form the foundation for your body and mind to be able to function at all. You can't do anything without this foundation being at least somewhat solid. Take care of it.

Depending on how much time you have to prepare, do some prep work so that you know that at least some of these things are covered. Stock up on basic food, toiletries, and paper goods. On that horrible night, when you have nothing else to give, you will thank me when you find that frozen dessert in the freezer or know that you have the ingredients to make your favorite chocolate chip cookies. Have at least a few hundred dollars in your car and your house. I once needed gas as I came back to Seattle from

Eugene, only to discover that I had forgotten my wallet in Oregon. I had a few dollars cash in the car and was able to make it home.

I hate pumping gas. I know hate is a strong word, but I really do hate getting gas. You may have other situations like this that, under normal circumstances, you can get away with. Not now, my friend. Just stop and get the damn gas when you get to a quarter of a tank. That way, you never need to even question if you have enough gas to make it anywhere if there is an emergency. Again, the added stress of having to fill up on your way to the hospital after you have gotten a call that something happened to your parent is just not worth it.

Make a list of the supplies, food, cash, and so on that you and your family will need that would be easier to stock up on now, rather than have to worry about getting later.

Here is an example:

- $50 cash in the car
- $500 cash at the house
- Frozen food
- Dry good foods for pantry
- Shampoo, conditioner, and other vital hair products
- Soap

- Toilet paper
- Laundry detergent and softener
- Basic cleaning supplies
- Toothpaste and floss
- Shaving supplies
- Wine
- Pet food
- Medication, if possible
- Special treats—but only if you won't eat them regularly

If you have sufficient means, go ahead and prepay any bills that you can pay, if not on automatic payments. Anything you can do now to minimize your stress and reduce time spent later on, do it. Prepay insurance, utilities, mortgage, and so on.

You may have other ideas on how to prepare for you surviving during this time. Go for it.

WHAT DO YOU NEED TO FUNCTION?

Functioning is a step up from survival. It is what you need in order to think clearly and do all that needs to be done, at least to satisfactory levels. What needs to be taken care of so that you are not distracted from taking care of the business at hand? For instance, my functioning ability diminishes greatly when my environment is physically chaotic. I don't do well with messes around me, clutter, dirty dishes hanging out, stuff not put away, or too much stuff around me. In a cluttered or chaotic environment, my anxiety skyrockets.

I can function well, even in a hut with a dirt floor in the jungle, as long as there isn't clutter and it is clean. (And yes, I have functioned in a hut with a dirt floor in the jungle before.)

I don't function at all when I get too hungry or tired. I can tolerate a lot, but don't mess with my food or my sleep. It isn't pleasant. I don't function well when I have eaten a bunch of crap the day before or had too much wine. It just makes functioning the next day very difficult. My best friend, Leigh, is extremely sensitive to sound. She doesn't function well in a loud environment, whereas my son, Jonathan, on the other hand, swears he can't work without headphones on, listening to things online that would drive me nuts. So what do you need in order to function to a satisfactory degree?

What makes you most comfortable while on vacation or staying with relatives? Without these things, you won't die, but you do function far better.

Here is my list:

- Good black and green tea. At least a cup in the morning, but preferably a pot. Yes, this needs to be high-quality tea. So, when I travel, I take my own tea with me.
- Tons of water every day
- Berries almost every day
- Quality soap, my shampoo and conditioner
- Glass of red at least once or twice a week
- Clean sheets every week
- Clothing that fits so that I don't have a hit to the gut when I try to put something on and it is too small
- Some form of physical activity at least five times a week. Even a twenty-minute walk or ten minutes of stretching a day. Something to move my blood around.
- Being in nature at least a few times per month, preferably on a hike, sitting in a forest, or at a beach
- Not having something that is going to be distracting, such as too much root grow-out; chipped toenail polish; a dog that needs a bath; that one long hair on my chin; trash that needs to be taken out; a dirty car; or other things that are just going to annoy me
- A tidy desk at work
- An accurate and up-to-date calendar
- In bed at 9:00 to 9:30 every night
- The lawn mowed before it is too shaggy
- The car interior tidy
- Being on time
- No computer or screen time after 8:00 p.m.

So, what do you need to function? Be honest with your-self, and don't judge it; just make your list. These tasks or things are what you need to stock up on, calendar, or guard so that you can function at your best level during this time. If being in nature is on the list, calendar it. If certain grooming is on your list, make appointments for the next six months now. For other items, just make a mental note that this item is important to your function-ing ability, and thus it is vital that you take care of it.

I can't emphasize how important it will be to calendar these activities. Even if you have to write "stretch" every day in your calendar, at least you will know that your vital function was done that day. Calendaring will save you from having to think every day about what you need to do to function better. While normally you wouldn't have a problem remembering to make a hair appointment, when you are under this much additional stress, it is easy to forget. If it is calendared, you don't have to think about it and you will relax knowing that it will be taken care of.

Simplify, Simplify, Simplify

Simplifying your life as much as possible will go a long way toward easing your burdens on this journey. You may find that your life works so much better when it is simpler that you keep simplifying after this experience ends. My home life is about as simple as it can possibly be now, after a long time period of being miserable with a far more complex life.

I have known since my teens that I work best with simple. I don't do well being overloaded. Yet I am creative, ambitious, and go a mile a minute. I also have a bit of an entrepreneurial spirit in me. I want to do a whole lot in this lifetime and I have done a whole lot in my forty-eight years.

I come up with ideas for new products and new businesses on a regular basis. I used to think that if I had a good idea that I should run with it. I have put tens of thousands of dollars into ventures but never stuck them out long enough for them to work, as I was on to the next thing. At one point, I planned out buying and renovating a ten-thousand-square-foot dilapidated chateau in France to have an Airbnb. Then it grew to five. You get the idea.

I love homes, specifically old homes. I have fully renovated two of them. There is nothing simple about renovating an old home. This passion has nearly bankrupted me. There is nothing simple about having a cash flow issue and a home that still doesn't have walls.

Simplifying one's life is "simple," and it is hard to do, especially if things are rather complex. It is about honoring all parts of yourself but keeping those parts as simple as possible at any given moment. Simple helps keep you balanced and helps you get back to balance if it starts going off. Then you can add a bit more complexity bit by bit to keep the balance.

Having too much complexity in one's life keeps one off balance and one can't get that balance back without simplifying. One of my three-month obsessions many years ago was pottery. I never have even really liked pottery. In any event, it was a fun activity for a bit. There is something meditative about being in the moment with the clay, the water, and the wheel. To make a clay piece, you take a piece of clay and shape it with your hands to make it appear to be symmetrical. When you are learning, it is best to start with a smaller piece of clay. Then you put it in the center of the wheel. It looks centered, but it isn't—not by a long shot. So, you start the wheel and your first job is to "cup" the clay to try to get the edges symmetrical and the clay balanced. It takes some experience to learn the feeling of when you have the clay balanced. Then you begin the process of forming your piece, little by little.

The tricky part is that you must be 100 percent focused on still feeling the piece to make sure it remains balanced. If it isn't, you need to fix it immediately—if you are able. Once it gets to a point, which is extremely fast and unpredictable, there is no "fixing" it and it will collapse. If it gets too much—too complicated—you have to literally start over and go back to simplicity. It is very disappointing when your piece is actually coming along, you are really proud of it, and it gets off balance and can't be fixed at the last stage of throwing it. All of that work and your masterpiece down the drain. You just have to start at the beginning.

Keeping things as simple as possible during this time will help you tune into when you are getting off balance so that you can correct course before you collapse or really start dropping balls. We have all been there, when you have a lot on your mind and you begin to forget things, start dropping things, or breaking things when you normally don't—because your mind is elsewhere, forgetting appointments, and so on. When you are going through this time period, those things are going to happen. However, the simpler your life is, the less damage that will be done and the fewer balls that will be dropped. If you get completely overwhelmed because you have an overly complex life, then when balls start to be dropped, it will snowball, and you will feel demoralized.

Let's simplify as much as we can so that you don't get to that point, or if you do, you can bounce back and balance more quickly. If ever you are going to do it, now is the time. I will go more into self-care further on in the book. For now, start to think about and maybe write down ways that you can start to simplify your life. It doesn't have to be extreme, but do something immediately to simplify.

Your house is supposed to be your safe place and your sanctuary. You are going to need it to be that more than ever. You are going to have a lot of chaos in your life. It will benefit you a lot to have your home as decluttered and serene as possible. The last thing you need after a very long and hard day and evening, when you are physically and emotionally exhausted, is to not be able to find something easily in your home because it is so jampacked with crap.

One of the most effective and fastest ways to simplify is to declutter. If there is any anger, anxiety, or frustration when you get dressed in the morning, maybe it is because you have too many clothing choices or a closet full of clothing that doesn't make you feel great or that doesn't fit. We wear clothes every day. This issue, therefore, will be a daily irritant unless you deal with it. Same goes for too much stuff in your house. So, one of the first things I would advise you to do is take a few hours or a day and purge. Get rid of the clothing you don't wear, doesn't fit, or you don't feel great in. You are going through a tough time and the last thing you need is to feel like crap because you are busting out of those pants or feel dowdy in that sweater.

A warning: don't purge everything quickly and then feel empty and turn around and use shopping as a coping mechanism. Many people find comfort in shopping.

I believe it is a false comfort and can be a destructive comfort, but people still use it as a comfort, nonetheless. Be careful with this one. You don't need the further complication of more stuff, more clutter, and more financial stress. Nor do you have the time.

Here are some other pretty easy things to simplify that will make a big difference, as they will cut down on the stimulation you are facing daily.

- Purge.
- Delete apps, messages, texts, and so on that you no longer need. You look at your phone many times a day, and it is going to be better for your brain to not see so many apps or messages.
- Clear out your car every day, every time you get home.
- Toss receipts immediately. Absent a big purchase, there is no reason to keep them.
- Unsubscribe to most of the emails you get. Again, this is just wasted time and stimulation you don't need at any time, much less now.
- Purge.
- Cancel services you don't need or use anymore.
- Fold and put your clothing away as soon as it is out of the dryer.
- Keep a healthy snack with you always.
- Purge (again).

If possible, resign from that professional committee that you are on, or the three. Do you really enjoy it anyway? At the very least don't agree to be on any more or take on any more duties. The first time my father was really ill, I resigned as chairperson of a committee in a business group I was in. I didn't know what the next year would entail, but I knew I didn't have the time or energy for a one-year commitment to a major project. It was more difficult than I thought to send that email from his hospital room. I felt like a quitter and that I was letting people down. But I did it and immediately felt relief. Somehow the group managed to almost immediately find a great replacement and pulled off a wonderful event. Still not sure how they did it without me, but they did.

Now is not the time to take on a big life project (other than simplifying life). Now is not the time to go back to school, try to lose sixty pounds, or build a house. You have enough on your plate, and all of those things will be there in six months—or whenever.

Your ability to say "no" during this time is one of the critical ingredients to keeping your sanity during this time. No to volunteer "opportunities;" no to that extra project at work; no to that football party or holiday party that you don't really want to go to anyway. It is okay even to say no to a friend coming over when you just want to be alone and read a book or stare at the wall. You are not obligated to spend your time doing something you don't want to do socially. You just aren't. In life, but especially now, if your answer is not an immediate "hell yes," then it should be a "no." You do not have the time, energy, or mental power to say yes to things that you don't feel in your heart.

Life is forcing you to run a marathon—whether you have trained or not. That is 26.2 miles that you will need to run, walk, or crawl. Every time you take something away to simplify your life, you are helping your body prepare for this marathon. You are giving it healthy food, training, good shoes, and sufficient time. Every time that you add something to your plate, you are cutting off part of one of your two legs. You are making a difficult situation ten times worse.

Do a hard examination when you find yourself telling someone, "I'm just so busy." We will get to time management later on, but sometimes we keep our lives complex and busy so that we are distracted from uncomfortable feelings. When my friend Linsey's mother was dying, she was married but didn't have children at the time. She had a solid career in which she was in complete control over her time, how many clients she worked with, and so on. Even though it was her "slow" time of year, she was still working twelve-hour days, six or seven days a week. During this time, I would ask her how she was doing, and without blinking her response was always "Oh I'm fine;

I am just so busy." I love my friend dearly *and* she has a habit of overworking. I know her well enough to be fairly confident that at least part of the reason she overworks is so that she doesn't have to deal with feelings she doesn't want to deal with.

I know it sucks even to think about losing a parent. It hurts like hell and I don't blame anyone for wanting to soften that hurt, avoid it, ignore it, or try to stuff it down with food, shopping, or wine. I get it. I also get that it doesn't work. That pain isn't going anywhere. If you don't deal with it, "it" will start leaking out in ways that are really unhealthy and can screw your life up. We have all had that work colleague who let their pain spill out in the form of snapping at people or just being an asshole. I have actually said many times, "Wish he would just go get therapy like the rest of us." (Not really joking here.)

So, when you want to cry, cry. When you want to scream, scream. It is healthy to sit and cry for hours at a time and "do nothing." You are doing something—something important and extremely productive. You are processing pain in a healthy manner and in a way that won't fuck you up later on. Don't cheat yourself from processing what you need to process in the name of being busy.

WHAT, IF ANYTHING, DO YOU OWE YOUR PARENTS AND WHY? WHAT ARE YOU WILLING TO GIVE?

Your automatic response to this question may be, "Huh? I owe them everything; they are my parents. It is my duty to take care of them, no matter what that takes." Others have the view that they owe their parents nothing. Everyone must think about and answer this question for herself or himself. But it is important to think about and answer, in order to answer the next question.

What are you willing to give? The problem is that if you don't have this answered, you will probably over-give, get burned out, and be resentful. I can almost promise you that you will snap at your parents during this time, and get frustrated and angry. I would start to question your sanity if you didn't have these reactions at times. You shouldn't have resentment if you are not over-giving. Or if you are only giving out of shame or because you feel pressured to do so.

You might have also had really shitty parents. Many people do. I want to be crystal clear here. You do *not* owe anyone your mental or emotional health. If someone is toxic or unhealthy for you, you don't owe them your time, energy, emotions, or anything else that is going to harm you, even if they are dying. My biological mother is not good for me. Having her in my life brought a lot of turmoil, anxiety, and hurt and was just not healthy for me. I haven't had direct contact with her in nearly ten years. That hasn't stopped her from continuing to shoot arrows at me through other family members, though. I have thought often of what I would do if I knew she was dying. I still don't have an answer, but I know that I don't owe her, or anyone else, anything that will bring toxicity into my life.

My adoptive, that is, "real" mother was not toxic. She had her issues but was not toxic. I did "owe" her and was going to do right by her. When my mother moved into assisted living, we knew fairly early on things were deteriorating quickly. I made the decision to give her my everything, other than my most basic needs, my son's most basic needs, and the energy necessary to not commit malpractice at work. If my business imploded, then so be it; I would rebuild. If I got through this time period alive myself, my son doing what he needed to be doing, my home intact, and with my law license, then that was fine. Anything else was a bonus.

Now, luckily, I came out of the experience with my business bruised but still standing. I could not have given it everything like I did if the journey had been much longer than it was. Your "give" should be proportional to what the facts actually call for at any given time.

My "give" for my father was a bit more of a roller coaster. When he first became really sick, I had literally given a workshop on dealing with older parents two weeks before. I had discussed what one is willing to "give" and the importance of the same. I laugh now, as when I was sitting in his ICU room, I had to go back and look at my notes for that workshop, as everything I had just taught was nowhere to be found in my brain.

It was evident that he would not be able to work anymore. At first, I thought, "Okay, I will sell my house, get licensed in Montana, and move to Colstrip to take care of him. My two brothers, who live there, can't take care of him; they have their own lives and shouldn't be burdened." The fact was that they were perfectly capable of caring for him. I didn't want my two single brothers to be burdened with caring for him, but I was willing to move my entire life to care for him in Colstrip, Montana. See the problem here? A friend quickly slapped me out of that one. She gently questioned whether there may, just maybe, be a solution that was not so extreme.

The next step was to get my home in Seattle to the point where my dad could live with me. I lived in an old home, with stairs and one full bath. I knew that if we shared a bathroom my father's death would come far sooner than necessary. So I got to work fast on a remodel of the upstairs to make a powder room into a full bathroom and a small bedroom into a master suite. Not the simplest of solutions, but it would work.

A few months later, my brothers and dad even came out and my brothers helped with the remodel, with my dad "supervising." By that time, my dad had been out of the hospital for a few months and was feeling much better. He already wasn't following doctors' orders by failing to use his oxygen 24/7, as well as not using equipment at night to breathe. By the time my home was ready for my dad, his health had improved. The idea of him living in my relatively small home in Seattle, without much of a yard and far away from nature, was not sitting well with me, though. Given his recovery, he could be living with me for years. The idea of moving kept popping up in my head.

I had been thinking about moving from Seattle for years, for various reasons unrelated to my father. So, in the fall of that year I listed my home, sold it in a day, and moved to Texas. I was in the beginning of renovating a 1940s farmhouse on 2.3 acres in rural Texas, not a simple lifestyle, when my dad got sick again. Now we all agreed he really couldn't go back to work. So I put the renovation into high gear and got it done in five and a half months.

By the time the house was ready for him, my dad had rallied, but not as high as the previous year. I finished the home in May. He didn't want to come down, as Texas was too hot in the summer. He would come out in the fall. As fall began to approach, my dad started to talk about hunting in October and November. You can see where I am going here. At first blush, it would appear that my dad didn't want to come out. That isn't the case. As much as I am a planner, my dad was not. Trying to pin him down to a date or time that wasn't within the next hour was harder than catching a greased pig.

Meanwhile, life on the farm was not going well for me. I hated it. I felt totally isolated; taking care of 2.3 acres is a lot of work, and not the fun kind. I was doing regular battle with snakes, spiders, mosquitos, and scorpions. Building a higher-end practice in a rural area in Texas was not going well either. The driving back and forth to the city was killing me. I had underestimated how much of a city girl I was and had overromanticized farm life.

I had also just built a freaking home for my father who had yet to even see it. This wasn't working, and it wasn't going to work. I wanted to move to Austin, but what about my dad? I really had to think about this one. I didn't owe my dad a farm. I would be in a far healthier financial situation to live in the city, as I could make money. I would live in an apartment until I figured out where in the city I wanted to live and get my practice up and running again. I would always have a bedroom for my dad, a comfortable place to live, and pay for his living expenses. He would need to make some adjustments and live in the city. The gun club was only five minutes away. He could deal with it.

I felt so at peace with this decision. When I discussed this with my dad, he teased a bit about having to have a smaller room in an apartment, but he was fine with it. Not that he had much choice.

So, as long as my father was alive, he would have a nice place to live with me. I would pay his living expenses, but not entertainment, not buy more guns, as he already had an arsenal (but one can evidently never have too many guns), and not pay for hunting. Those he could do on his own if he chose. I would physically take care of him as much as I was able and at home for as long as we were able. However, I was not going to neglect my practice to the point of wondering if it was going to make it or not. I wouldn't neglect my body to the point of gaining thirty pounds again.

I sold my home and planned to move to Austin. During the closing process, my dad got ill again. I closed on my house on a Thursday, moved into my apartment on Friday, and was in the ICU in Montana with my father on Tuesday. He died on Thursday. I am still glad I made the decisions I did about what to give my father that I did, even though he never ended up living with me.

YOUR "WHY"

What is your "why?" Your "why" is important, as you can

do anything with a good "why." Without it, doing things will be miserable and you will be resentful. If you are only doing something because you feel you have a duty to, then you are far more likely to have resentment. On paper, I didn't "owe" my father anything. He didn't take care of me growing up. He didn't raise me. I didn't meet him until I was twenty-three years old. My "why" is that I loved this man with all of my heart. My "why" is because since the first phone call, he loved me and treated me just like my brothers. My "why" is because he was one of the most important people in my life. He was my dad, and I was his little girl. A father had never loved a daughter more than my dad loved me. That was my "why," and that kept my head on straight.

Get your "why" sorted out sooner rather than later.

So, what are your personalized bare basics that you need to function? What is your oxygen that you can and will do once a week to refresh, breathe, and get yourself somewhat centered? What activities can you get off your plate? Could you declutter at home or work? When will you commit to yourself to do this? How else can you simplify your life, and what can you do right now? Every piece of sand that you remove will make a difference, I swear.

Think about and decide what, if anything, you will give to your parent and why. Set those boundaries now, even if just in your head, rather than in the middle of a crisis when you can't think clearly.

Your being clear on your "why" is going to be particularly important if your relationship with your parent has not been particularly healthy or happy. Unfortunately, there are many parents in the world who have not been good parents; some have been rather horrible parents. How one handles the death of a parent who is toxic is particularly delicate, as there will not be any second chances.

Chapter Three

THE TOXIC PARENT

———

*Forgiveness is releasing all hope that
things could have been different.*

—OPRAH WINFREY

I emailed my friend Philip to ask what he wishes he had
known before his parent died. This is what he wrote me.

*I wish someone had told me that nobody's well-being mat-
tered more than my own.*

I wish someone had told me how to handle the guilt.

*I wish someone had told me that it was okay to walk away
from a toxic parent, even when that parent is dying.*

I wish someone had given me permission to trust my gut on whether to communicate or not with my dying parent.

I wish someone had given me some guidance on just how much open honesty is necessary, helpful, or would tarnish my parent's final days.

I wish someone had told me how to recognize common patterns of emotional manipulation from a parent.

I wish someone had told me it was okay to be relieved after a parent's death.

I wish someone had told me to ask about my parent's life stories to learn from them and to be able to save them.

I'd tell someone one thing and one thing only: "Do your best for your dying parent. But you are only duty-bound to save yourself, not anyone else."

Like Philip, plenty of adult children have toxic parents. Regardless of what you call them: narcissist, toxic, selfish, personality disorder, emotionally abusive, or just plain assholes. People have this romantic notion that when people are faced with their own death that they will "see the light," apologize for their sins, and want to leave this earth in peace with their family. That has not been my experience. If you were raised by wolves, those wolves are not going to morph into sweet kittens just because they are dying. In fact, they might very well get meaner.

It is important to be honest with yourself about who your parent really is or is not and then respond accordingly. Yes, this is your last shot to heal some things with them, but you probably are not going to be successful. This may, however, be an incredible opportunity for you to do some difficult work and heal some of your own wounds, learn to create boundaries, and develop new skills.

First, recognize people's behavior for what it really is. You are not losing your mind. Emotional abusers are really skilled. Below is a list of behaviors that may or may not be familiar to you. If any of them hit a nerve, pay attention to that.

The emotional abuser:

- Humiliates you, alone or in front of others
- Blames you when called out on their behavior
- Belittles and trivializes your hopes, dreams, and accomplishments
- Tries to control you and your behavior
- Blames you for his problems
- Tries to make you doubt your sanity
- Lacks respect and points out your mistakes or shortcomings

- Isolates you from others
- Turns your words against you to their benefit
- Refuses to apologize
- Denies that they said something to you
- Guilt trips you
- Diminishes your problems or difficulties
- Repeatedly says things that they know upset you
- Expects you to prioritize them but doesn't prioritize you

What you can do to keep your sanity:

- Make it clear that a real apology is unconditional and to be followed by a change in behavior.
- Do not get in the ring with them. The only way to win an argument with someone who is emotionally abusive is to not engage in one with them. You simply cannot engage with them.
- Don't give in to their passive demands or requests for sympathy. Remind them that they are an adult and able to cope.
- Walk away.

Keep in mind that their superpower is manipulation. And they are great at it. Don't be surprised if others don't see it. They believe they are above the rules. When called out on their unethical, immoral, criminal, or just bad behavior, they react by being a victim or attacking the reporting party or actual victim. They make horrible parents and were horrible parents. They lacked basic empathy and the selfless nature that loving parenting requires. They met their own needs before their child's and felt totally justified in doing so.

They are emotionally needy, and their needs are a bottomless pit. That cup has no bottom. So pouring liquid into the cup will never do any good. They don't have conversations. They have competitions in order to manipulate, confuse, distort reality, control, and create drama. It is vital to remember that they will never change. Nor will they apologize. Not even when they are lying on their death bed.

So what do you owe them? You owe them the respect that any other human being deserves. Nothing more. You don't owe them your time, money, attention, or mental or emotional health. I would say that you owe yourself, and the rest of us, the duty to do the difficult work to heal so that you don't repeat this harmful behavior.

The best advice I have ever received on decision making was from Darren Hardy. When faced with decisions, frankly all life decisions, ask yourself this:

Am I more likely to say:

I wish I hadn't

or

I am glad I did?

Easy for me to say? My biological mother and I have not had contact in nearly ten years. On paper, she is a well-adjusted functioning adult. Nothing close to being diagnosed as a narcissist. Her behavior is not criminal, immoral, or even unethical. She is "nice." That is, until you do something she doesn't want you to do, don't do exactly what she does want, or challenge her in any way. She had no problems putting her own wants above my needs. She has no problem doing really mean and shitty things.

It took me well over a decade and some great mental healthcare to finally catch on to what she was doing and not engage with her when she would start in. Standing up to her has cost me siblings, aunts and uncles, cousins, and even my grandmother "sneaks" contact with me. I am the bad one. I am the one to be tossed from the tribe.

I do know the visceral longing to have a parent (even one who didn't raise me) put me first, do the right thing, and be a good parent. You want it so fucking badly. And you are not going to get it. And this is even though I had a great mom and overall a really good childhood. I can't imagine how it feels if this parent was your only mother or father.

I have thought many times of trying to reach out, again, before one of us dies. Each time I come to the same realization that nothing would be different, and when we were in contact it put me in some very bad places and was not good for me. It sucks to love someone and not be able to be around them because they are toxic in your life. But it is what it is. The sooner you accept that fact and establish healthy boundaries for yourself, the sooner you will get your sanity. Even if it means walking away.

Remember, you can't heal in the same environment that made you sick in the first place.

Chapter Four

WHAT YOU CAN EXPECT

—————

When you let go of your expectations, when you accept life as it is, you're free. To hold on is to be serious and uptight. To let go is to lighten up.

—RICHARD CARLSON, *DON'T SWEAT THE SMALL STUFF... AND IT'S ALL SMALL STUFF: SIMPLE WAYS TO KEEP THE LITTLE THINGS FROM TAKING OVER YOUR LIFE*

"Sorry you're dying, but I have shit to do." What kind of horrible person gets irritated for having to take their dying mother to the doctors? Me, I am that horrible person.

Guess what? You probably will have those same, or very similar, feelings at one point or another during this process. You can expect to feel a whole host of emotions, maybe within thirty minutes.

Every person is different, every family is different, and every situation is different. Your experience will be different in 101 ways from anyone else's. However, there are some common themes that continue to emerge with people who have gone through losing their parent. You might not have all of these challenges or experiences, but if you do, you will have some information ahead of time to help you navigate them.

So what can you expect during this process?

DEALING WITH MEDICAL PERSONNEL

I believe that the majority of people who enter the medical profession do so with good intentions, and most are great at what they do. If you choose a good facility and a reputable doctor, you should expect to be treated with kindness and respect. You should expect they will give you accurate information so that your parent can make intelligent decisions. You should expect to be seen at your appointment time or a reasonable number of minutes (no more than fifteen) thereafter.

You should also expect a heck of a lot of medical appointments, sometimes with many different medical professionals. They don't come to you or care much about your schedule. So, depending on your parent's health, you could be looking at appointments from once a month to several each week. Your parent is going to need transportation to and from each of those appointments. You are probably also going to want to attend at least some of them to get an accurate and complete summary of what is going on with your parent, as well as to make sure the doctor gets accurate and complete information from your parent.

For instance, my father was notorious for leaving out about 60 percent of what he was told by his doctors. He also had a selective memory when answering the doctor's questions. I get it; he didn't want to admit he ate those Krispy Kreme donuts or didn't use his oxygen all of the time. However, his doctors needed this information. So, after we caught on, either I spoke with the doctor or my brother went with him.

Going to the doctor with your parent, even if some of the time, serves several different purposes. If you have a stubborn parent, like my father, it provides your parent with accountability. He or she knows that you heard what the doctor said and will give him hell when he is tempted to go against the doctor's advice. This is especially true if lack of follow-through adversely affects your life. I am not saying punish your parent like a child, but it is totally valid to remind him or her that you are doing your part, and they need to do theirs. Gently, with love, not venom.

It also serves to remind the physician that someone else

is watching. Physicians are people, just like everyone else, and people do a better job when they know someone is keeping watch. It also serves to give them permission or guidance if your parent won't.

For instance, my mother was older, had been a nurse, and would always submit to authority or perceived authority. She never stood up for herself in her life. She did not even stand up for me in times when I desperately needed her to do so. When she had her second cancer diagnosis and we were on the third "trial" treatment (which was getting nowhere), I had a private talk with her physician. I told him that my mother had been a nurse, deferred to authority, and that if he told her to wear a tinfoil hat on her head, sing, and jump up and down, she would. Seriously, my mother would never say no to a physician. He could have kept her on trials, even with horrible side effects, until the day she died. I then told him that if the "next" trial really had some hope, then great, but if we were just throwing spaghetti at the wall to see if something would stick, then maybe we should think of another option, given the side effects of each new trial.

She had a great doctor who completely understood the situation and said that we were done with trying new and unproven treatments. I will forever be grateful to him for his common sense, kindness, and putting my mother first.

When one gets down to the place where your parent

needs twenty-four-hour care, you can, for the most part, expect the same kindness and competency from medical personnel. However, don't expect solid answers in as far as how long "this" is going to last, what happens next, and so on. As much as you want to know how long your parent will live, they just can't answer those questions. It is really frustrating. It is a real test to know that you need to do what you are doing and no one can tell you how long. It is like doing a plank or burpees and just being told to keep going indefinitely.

What you can expect from assisted care facilities is a bit different, even the really good and expensive ones. Keep in mind that most of the people who work at these facilities are good people, have too many patients to care for, are not paid well, and have to deal with a lot of shit, literally and figuratively.

They are not going to care for your parent as you would or probably as you would like. They will care for him or her much better if they know you are around a lot and watching them.

Trust Your Gut

There are amazing medical facilities and providers and really crappy ones. Many times, you don't have a choice in where your parent is seen, especially in an emergency.

Of course, doctors know a hell of a lot more than you do. I am not suggesting substituting your knowledge for theirs or not taking their advice. Even doctors who are not great know more than you do about medicine. With that said, pay attention and trust your gut. If something isn't making sense, question it. If the doctor is telling you it is time for your parent to be discharged, yet they don't look, sound, or feel any better than when they came in, that is something to question. My aunt complained to her primary physician about not feeling well for over a year. He continued to tell her nothing was wrong with her and finally implied that any fatigue was due to her being overweight. Well, she had been overweight for the last twenty years; why was she so fatigued now? No answer. By the time she saw another doctor she was in stage 4 cancer. She died within a few months.

My father had to go to the emergency room in another state while traveling. There was no question as to what was wrong with him as this was routine at this point. My dad complained to me that there was no communication in this hospital. The personnel had no idea what the other personnel had said to him or done. His care was subpar at best. He was discharged even though he still had pneumonia. Sure enough, he was back in the hospital, in intensive care in Montana within four days of being released from the first hospital. This was his last trip to the hospital.

I don't know what would have happened if the bad hospital had done their job and not released him until after his pneumonia had cleared, or whether my aunt would have beaten her cancer. What I do know is that neither of those situations passed the common sense smell test and both had permanent consequences. So if something seems off, question it and get a second opinion.

TIME

Time is the most valuable resource any of us has. It is so important that I have written an entire chapter on how to get the most of each twenty-four hours you have every day. For now, just know that your time will be constrained in ways you probably never have known. Your structure and schedule will be blown to bits, and you will need to adjust your expectations on how you are to spend your time on a regular basis. Had your day planned out? Going to get really important stuff done today? That was until you needed to run your mother to the ER. Now your entire day is blown to shit. Even if you were only there half of the day, it isn't like you are going to be able to concentrate well and get back to anything on your list that takes any concentration or focus.

The more you simplify life, the better you will be able to deal with these blowups, but they are going to happen nonetheless and blow your entire day—or more than one. It really is like going back to having infants or small children, when your time just didn't belong to you anymore—they were in charge of it. Be patient with yourself and try not to get frustrated when your best-laid plans go up in flames, again.

FEELINGS

The feelings that will come up in you are all over the map. I am not a mental health professional, and I still know that it is really important that you feel what you are feeling at the time, deal with it, and not try to ignore it or stuff it away.

You are going to feel totally overwhelmed and frustrated at the situation, at your parent, at others who don't "get" what you are going through, at medical personnel, at your kids, at your spouse, at your coworkers, at the driver in front of you, and at yourself. You will probably be irritable and snap more than normal. You may have some resentment at having to take care of your parent. At the same time, you may start to grieve, as you know you are losing your parent. You are losing any chance at all of those wonderful plans with him or her, or grieving what you have lost if they weren't a great parent. There isn't going to be another Christmas, Mother's Day, whatever. You are going to lose your parent, and that is a big deal. Your kids are losing their grandparent. Maybe you don't even have kids; your future kids will never have a grand-parent. A lot of crap is going to come up during this time. That old unresolved childhood crap—it's back. This is heavy stuff, my friend.

Again, you might be resentful. No parent is perfect, and many are far on the other side of perfect. Many times—most of the time—those issues have never been resolved. So you are busting your ass taking care of someone who didn't take great care of you. Yeah, those feelings can come up like a gusher, even if you think you had dealt with them.

Then you have the guilt. The guilt about your negative feelings, about being frustrated at your parent or others. The guilt about not being with your parent when you are at work. The guilt about not being at work when you are with your parent during the workday. No matter what you do, you are dropping the ball somewhere and feeling guilt about it.

There are some good feelings, though, too. When my mother was dying, I felt love for her like I had never felt before. I had always loved her, but this was a whole new level. We laughed over such simple things. I also felt so protective of her. No mama bear had anything on me. I did take good care of her, and I was proud of myself for that.

For some reason, the last month, when she was unconscious most of the time but could still squeeze my hand
and pucker up for a kiss, I started calling her Mama. I
had no idea why, as I had never called her that in my life.
I still don't know why I did. It just started coming out of
my mouth and felt right. When I talk to her now, even in
my head, I still call her Mama.

Same with my dad. I made a conscious effort to remember that my time with him was limited. I did my best
not to get annoyed when he would call me three times
a day, in the middle of work, just to talk about nothing
of importance. The last twenty-four hours with my dad
were indescribable. The communication in both of our
eyes was something I had never experienced with any
other person. I have never felt so much love going back
and forth before.

Be open to whatever feelings come your way. Work
through them as well as you can, as they are not going
anywhere.

Parent's Memory Lapses

Speaking of feelings, if your parent's memory starts to
go, get ready for some frustration, some good laughs,
and good stories. As we get older, all of us will experience memory problems. Not being able to remember

the name of your favorite author, where you put the car keys, and so on. The speed in which we can recall things starts to slow, even as early as the thirties. The key is to recognize the difference between the mental hiccups that occur naturally with age and the more serious lapses that affect our ability to function and can signal dementia or Alzheimer's disease. This is a real fear of many adults in their midlife. The fear is not misplaced either. By the time people are eighty-five, about half will develop dementia or Alzheimer's.

If your parent is having memory issues that are interfering with his or her functioning, such as getting lost in a familiar setting, forgetting to take medications, not being able to perform routine tasks, or not recognizing familiar faces or objects, then it is past the time to talk to their doctor.

When your parent starts telling you the same story over and over again, it can be very frustrating. Be patient. Your dad really doesn't remember that he has told you the story five times. Reminding him that he has done so—thus telling him that he is losing his memory and mind—isn't going to be helpful. No one wants to lose their memory or admit that they are doing so. I can't imagine how frightening it must be. No matter how frustrating it can be, don't lose your cool.

Keep a log, even just mentally, of the frequency and seriousness of the memory lapses. You will want to talk to your parent's doctor well before there is a safety issue or your parent doesn't recognize faces.

Depending on your parent's personality, at first these memory issues can be a bit funny, until they are not. Humor can help everyone deal with a horrible thing that is happening, to a point. It was fun for my brothers and me to tease my dad about his memory lapses, at the beginning. God knows we owed him some crap, as my dad was merciless about teasing us. However, when we realized that this was actually "a thing," it wasn't funny anymore, and we stopped. Now, we have good stories and can laugh about it.

My friend Jennifer's grandmother has Alzheimer's. She is a fine old-fashioned Southern lady. Grooming and having one's "face on" is as important as going to church. Recently, she used lipstick as an eyebrow pencil to fill in her eyebrows. She was as proud as could be. Of course, this is funny. She looked ridiculous. No, one doesn't burst out laughing in front of her, but yes, this will go down as one of the great Nana stories and still makes me laugh. Humor is a wonderful and healthy release if it doesn't hurt others.

Your Parent's Emotions and Outbursts

During this time, it can be easy to get irritated with your

parent. Believe me. Please do try to keep in mind that your parent is going through their own crap. He or she is the one who is dying. I have absolutely no idea how scary this journey is when you are the one who is actually going to die. When you are the one who is leaving everyone you love and everything you know for the unknown. Regardless of one's religious beliefs, none of us really knows what happens after we die. Of course your parent may be frightened.

My mother was a very religious person who "knew" where she was going. She was still scared and still fought hard to live.

It is normal for your parent to lose his or her temper and get snappy. They are also in pain, dependent, tired, having trouble getting around, and probably on a lot of medication that can also affect mood. Don't take it personally. I know how I feel even when I have a simple cold. I am really not the most pleasant person to be around.

I think, in my entire life, my mother may have snapped at me five times. I don't recall her ever yelling at me. I can't imagine her snapping at anyone else. Yet one day when I went to see her, a nurse commented about my mother's "temper." What? My mother doesn't have a "temper." Well, she did now. There were only a few more times when my mother got snappy with people, but it was still completely out of her norm.

On the other hand, my father's temper was legendary. When Mike Johnson was mad, "hot" as he said, you and everyone else in a mile radius knew it. It didn't take a lot for him to get "hot," and it took a while for him to cool down. This was especially true when he couldn't communicate. There were three times when he was on a ventilator. He was pretty "hot" that his arms were strapped down to the bed. This is standard procedure, as it is human nature to want to get the ventilator tube out, and people try to take it out if their arms are not strapped to the bed. No amount of calmly talking to my dad made that situation better. At one point he even flipped me off. I was so shocked I began to cry. The nurse told me it was totally normal and he wasn't in his right mind, given the drugs.

Then he would calm down a bit and try to tell us what he wanted. It didn't take long for us to get some paper. He tried to write, but we couldn't make out his handwriting (which wasn't great on a good day), and he would get more frustrated. It took a lot of patience and effort for him to communicate even the most basic requests.

The second time he was ventilated, the nurse had told him that they were going to be taking it out in about twenty minutes. There was an emergency in the ICU and that twenty minutes was now twenty minutes overdue. My dad pushed the call button a few times, but no one came. Since he was Mike Johnson, he broke his wrist restraints and pulled the tube out himself. With a ventilator there is a rather large tube that goes down one's throat and it has a balloon at the end of it. When the tube is removed, the nurse deflates the balloon before attempting to pull the tube out. Removing the tube is incredibly painful, even with the balloon deflated. When one removes a ventilator tube, DIY style, the balloon is *not* deflated as one is pulling the tube out of one's throat. Imagine giving birth through your throat. That is how mad my dad was.

Pack your patience, people, this is going to be a bumpy ride.

Wish You Were Dead

When you are exhausted, your life has been put on hold, you are dropping balls all over the place, and your parent is in pain, is grouchy, and has little to no quality of life, it is totally natural to just want "this" over. It is a no-win battle. Yes, you want your parent to live forever, and you want this horrible time to be over with. Or you were raised by wolves and are ready for your parent to die. Regardless, this time really sucks. I would look twice at you if you said everything was "fine" or you were not willing to admit that this was a really difficult time, or at least willing to admit to yourself that it will be nice when "it" is over. Then a millisecond later you remember that when this time is over, you won't ever see your parent again, and the guilt and pain start anew.

If you are having thoughts that scare or shame you, don't be too hard on yourself. You are not a monster, nor do those thoughts mean you don't love your parent. Just feel the feelings; don't get stuck on them. Take a walk and a deep breath and get back to putting one foot in front of the other.

HOSPICE

Before my mother was getting close to dying, I had no idea what hospice was. Hospice is defined as a home providing care for the sick, especially the terminally ill. Hospice comes to the patient and is free of charge as long as the patient is Medicare Part A-entitled. As part of it, a nurse is provided during the final phase of life to focus on the patient's comfort and quality of life.

Hospice is really a team of people. I have yet to find a "list" of the tasks that hospice personnel are charged with doing. Instead, I will tell you my experience.

Here is what all of this meant in my mother's case. An

angel nurse was sent to us, named Michelle. She was one of the most compassionate and patient people I had ever met. She answered all of my questions, over and over again. She acted as a communication liaison between myself and my mother's doctor. She acted as a second pair of eyes and ears at the assisted living facility for me. At one time, there was an issue with my mother's care. She knew exactly what to do and was with me during a meeting with the owner of the facility. She talked me out of the decision to just take my mother to my house and care for her there. She did this in a logical but very caring way, so that I felt good about my decision.

She was there day and night for me to call on. She arranged a few nights, and I was offered more, of respite care. Respite care is when a hospice volunteer spends time with your parent, even spending the night, to give you a break. She was the one who told me it was time to move my mom into a hospital setting. She was the one who called me and told me my mom had died. She was the one who had opened the windows "to let my mom's soul out of the room" in accordance with an old Swedish tradition. She sat with me until I was ready for her to go that night. She checked on me afterwards. She made the arrangements for my mom to be picked up by the funeral home.

She was my guide, and I have absolutely no idea how I

would have gotten through that time without her. I really don't. She acted as my counselor, my mom's advocate, my mother's caregiver, and my guide, and was amazing.

I have spoken with many other people who have experience with hospice, and I have yet to hear a negative thing. Not to say that there are none, as hospice workers are people, just like the rest of us, but I would feel very comfortable saying that your life will be easier when hospice gets involved with your parent. Yes, it means that all acknowledge that this is the end of life, although it doesn't mean imminent death, but bringing in hospice really is a gift to the patient and their family.

What Does Death Look Like?

"Mom, it is time to go." This is what I said to my mother, gently but firmly, the day before she died. My mother's death was unusual. Two hospice personnel indicated that her death was the worst and second-worst death they had ever seen. My God, she fought it tooth and nail.

There was no simple going to sleep and not waking up for my mom. This woman, who had not been a fighter during her life, was making up for it now.

Several times, I spent the night thinking that there was no way she would make it through the night. Yet she did.

One morning she woke up, looked at me, and said, "What are you doing here"? I replied, "What are you doing here?"

I do best with a lot of information. The doctors and nurses really did their best and were patient with me even when I asked the same questions over and over again. I wanted to know the process, the timeline, what would happen next and when. They had some idea, but my mom kept surprising them. One thing would happen, and they would say, "Okay, when that happens, death usually occurs within four days." Okay, we have four days. *Nope.* Four days would come and go and then six. The next thing that would happen, we would repeat the cycle. Then they just stopped telling me anything, as she wasn't following the rules.

She had long since stopped eating. Nurses had even stopped giving her the water-soaked swabs in her mouth, as the water was just prolonging her life. It really is amazing how fast one loses weight when one is not having any food or water.

I pray that your parent goes easily, sitting at a creek's edge surrounded by friends, like Senator McCain did recently. Because the alternative is horrible, absolutely horrible.

So horrible that if you don't want to know, then stop reading this section and skip to the next section. If you are like me and want to know what could be ahead, then keep reading.

Watching someone die slowly is horrible, interesting, and beautiful all at the same time. Even as morbid as it was, it was fascinating watching a body slowly shut down. The weight loss is dramatic. We have all seen the photos and videos of skeletons at Nazi prison camps. Think of that and far worse. There is really no muscle left. The skin has a weird yellow tint and is taut.

The body's systems are shutting down one by one. It isn't like a light switch, though. The body is fighting to stay alive and so each system is intermittent. So, when my mother's nervous system was sputtering, she would seem to experience shocks and have almost mini-convulsions. It would only last for seconds, and it was absolutely horrible.

During this phase, blood pressure drops dramatically and breathing patterns are irregular.

One sure sign that death is imminent is what they call the "death rattle." When you hear it, it is unmistakable. It is a gurgling sound in the dying and unconscious person's throat. It is the end-stage wet respiration that occurs when secretions build up in the person's throat and airway. Normally a person can clear these secretions automatically. However, when one is unconscious, one can't clear the airway. These secretions build up and cause a loud, rattling sound when air passes through the airway. Know that they are not causing discomfort to your loved one, just you.

They are generally seen as a sign that the end of this journey is close.

Watching my mother die in such a horrible way was excruciating. She had not been conscious for over a week. I still talked with her, assuming she could hear and understand me. She would moan when she was in pain, and when I would talk to her, she moaned less. So, we were going with the idea that she could hear me. The last four days of her life, she was on two hundred milligrams of morphine an hour and still moaning in pain. Two hundred milligrams can cause a death by overdose.

A few days before she died, I talked to her about who was waiting for her and that my son and I would be okay without her. I was trying to give her permission to go, as I really couldn't understand why she was fighting so hard, given her beliefs.

The next day, I got a bit firmer and told her that this is not how she would have wanted to die and that she needed to go be with Grandma. That we were fine, would see her soon, and she needed to go.

My mother was dying of everything. She had not had food for well over a week, so she was dying of starvation. She had not had water for well over a week, so she was dying of dehydration. Cancer was ravaging her bones, and she was dying of pain. She was in immense pain, starving, had bed sores even though we moved her frequently, and her skin was so frail and fragile one was scared to touch her, as it could break and tear, literally.

During this time, I would look at my mom's pillow. It could solve everything. She would be out of pain, and this would be over. In those moments, I really didn't even care about the legal ramifications to me. It never went beyond brief thoughts, as I knew that that is not what my mother would want, but boy, I still thought about it.

I don't think that any medical personnel would have blinked an eye, given my mother's state. I don't know how I would have felt afterwards or if it would have haunted me forever. I didn't have to find out, as I knew how my mother felt about euthanasia. She wanted to go naturally when her time was up and not a second earlier, even if this condition is what that meant.

There is also a beauty to watching someone die, as odd

as that may sound. They are about to go somewhere you have never been and know nothing about. To be with someone during their last moments on Earth is a tremendous privilege.

The night my mother died, I had shortened my visit, as I just couldn't take it. She wasn't responsive at all, and her body was jolting. I walked out of her room and couldn't even talk to the nurse to tell her why I was leaving. I remember putting my hands up and mouthing that I just couldn't do it. I got the call that my mom had died about an hour and a half later.

It is very common for people to wait to die until their loved one is out of the room. I have heard many stories about people not dying until everyone goes to get a meal, or even to the bathroom. Don't ask me why, that is just what happens. I have a friend who used to own a funeral home. It was just an accepted fact that there would be a post-Christmas "rush," as people would fight and wait to die until after the holidays.

When someone dies, if there is any waste left, they will release it upon death. So don't be alarmed if your loved one defecates after death or there are unpleasant smells even shortly after death. Also, although the body has shut down, sometimes the nervous system still has a jolt or two left. It is not completely uncommon for lips to move;

there have even been stories of people who are dead sitting up.

My father's death was not so dramatic. We were told that after removing the ventilator, he could go immediately or not until four hours later. I got such a gift when my father opened his eyes after we had the ventilator removed. We looked at each other for a good minute before he closed his eyes again. My father didn't die for eight and a half hours. But when he did, it was totally peaceful, and the only reason I knew it was coming was his numbers started to drop dramatically. I will say it again, it is actually something so beautiful to be with someone when they are dying, much less holding their hand when they die. It is a spiritual experience that I can't describe. I am just so thankful I got to experience it with my dad.

Every death is different, and it is impossible for anyone to say when your parent will die or what it is going to look like. I think that a balanced approach to knowledge is a good thing in this arena. No, you don't need to do much research on the signs of imminent death—don't get obsessive but do know the basics so that you aren't alarmed when you see them.

A SPECIAL MESSAGE FOR MEN

In my experience, men still feel that they need to be the

stoic who can handle anything. What I would say to a man whose parent is dying is that this is your damn mom or dad, and this sucks and is going to hurt, and we cry when it hurts. *No one* is going to think any less of you, regardless of how old you are.

When I was a young litigant, I appeared nearly every day in front of Judge T, a tall, white-haired jurist who had been practicing since the earth cooled. He was as cool as a cucumber and didn't lose his temper. He had seen it all and remained unfazed. He was well into his seventies and still putting in the long and hard days of a trial court judge. His mom passed away during my time in his courtroom. When he returned to work, I approached the bench after the calendar was over to tell him how sorry I was for his loss.

At first, he was same old Judge T. "Oh yes, well, thank you." Then the tears started. Ohhh, that was tough. I will never forget what he said: "It doesn't matter how old you are, she is still your mom."

So, yes, she is still your mom. You don't have to "handle" anything.

RELIEF

I cannot say this enough. Depending on the journey, you

may feel relief when your parent dies. This is okay. Now go back and read that again, and again, and again. Type it out five hundred times and put sticky notes all over your home if you need to.

Again, this is normal, and you are not a horrible person. Seeing your parent moving toward death sucks and it is totally natural to be relieved when that experience is over. You may also be exhausted and completely drained. It is a relief to think that you may get to sleep again at some point in your life.

My mother died in the evening. That night, I gave instructions for my legal assistant so that I didn't have to worry about the office for a few days. I then went home and was asleep before my head hit the pillow. I don't think I shed a tear, and I am a crier. I don't really remember the next three days, other than I know I slept and slept and slept. After three days, I remember looking up to the sky and talking to God, or whoever, and saying, "Okay, I have slept, you can bring her back now." Of course, it doesn't work like that, does it?

If your parent was toxic, then of course you are going to feel relief. There would be something wrong with you if you didn't. It is okay. It is healthy. You have nothing to feel bad about.

Think about your expectations of this process. What, if anything, do you expect? Are those expectations reasonable? Do you have control over the people who are involved? What can you control and what is out of your control?

If you are a type A person or like to be in control at all, I would highly suggest, like slap you across the face suggest, that you let go. You are not in control of this, not in any way, shape, or form. Don't try to fight the process or your feelings. Just relax and move through it.

Chapter Five

TIME MANAGEMENT, ACTUALLY SELF- MANAGEMENT

Behavior is the mirror in which everyone shows their image.
—JOHANN WOLFGANG VON GOETHE

Anyone can tell you all about what is important to them, but how they spend their time and their money is proof, beyond a shadow of a doubt, of their true priorities.

People lie, behavior doesn't. When one sees someone's checking account, it is instantly evident what their true priorities are.

Even more telling is how people spend their time. Don't

tell me that your health is important to you and yet you haven't exercised once this week. Don't tell me your marriage or children are important to you when you haven't spent even two hours talking with either this week without your smartphone or TV on.

Okay, you can flip me off now. The truth hurts, my friend.

I know, I know, you have a lot of responsibilities. You have kids. You have a spouse and a boss. You have a high-demand career. And now you have a parent to take care of. People need to be able to reach you outside of office hours. You must multitask, or you would get nothing done. If you didn't multitask, talk on the phone when driving, and do the other 101 things every ten minutes, your life would fall apart.

So how is that working for you? You are probably getting a lot done. Are you getting what is really important done? Are you busy for busyness's sake but not moving anywhere?

What if there were a way in which you could work less, get more results, have some free time, and not have guilt about how you are spending your time? Sound too good to be true? It really is doable. It is simple, but hard.

If you implement even a few of the ways in which I learned

to modify my behavior, you will be ahead of the game. I would contend that, when caring for another adult, these behavior changes will get you, your family, your career, and your other relationships through this time relatively unscathed and without unnecessary guilt.

When caring for another adult, your time is going to be taxed as never before. Whatever you thought of your time-management skills before, you are going to have to not only bring your A game, but learn a whole new A game. You are in the big leagues now, baby, and whether you start dropping balls, missing appointments, not getting enough sleep, and surviving is largely going to be dependent on how you manage your time and manage yourself.

I have always taken pride in my time-management skills. I can generally get more done by 10:00 a.m. than most people get done all day. However, I was continually not meeting my important goals. I was busy and it felt good to get a lot of things crossed off of my to-do lists, but I wasn't accomplishing what I had told myself was important. I was managing my time but not managing my behavior.

This chapter is largely based on the work of Darren Hardy and is about how to use the twenty-four hours that you get every day to meet your goals, as well as your new responsibilities, and to be able to prioritize what is really important to do with your time.

This is the information that I really wish I had when I was taking care of my mom. This information would have made my life, and the lives of the people around me, much better during that time. This is the information that I use now, and I have been able to increase my productivity, increase my rest and down time, add fun into my life, and focus on what is really important. This way of managing my behavior is the only reason that I am able to sit down and write this book every day.

I know that when one is in survival mode, it can be next to impossible to even be able to tell what is important. It is too big, too overwhelming, so we focus on the small. With these tools, you will be able to focus on what needs to be done and when.

The bottom line is that you have the same twenty-four hours each day that Bill Gates has, Justice Ruth Bader Ginsburg has, and everyone else has. You don't have more responsibilities than anyone else. What you do with that twenty-four hours is what is going to make or break your life at any time in life, especially now.

ONE TASK ONLY, PLEASE

I know I am going to get flak for this one, but there is no such thing as being able to multitask. I could never "multitask" and felt like something was wrong with me when others would brag about their ability to multitask. Study after study is now demonstrating that multitasking is simply not possible. Your brain is only able to focus on one thing at a time. So when you are multitasking, what you are doing is cognitively switching back and forth between activities. You are not completing either cognitive function, as you keep switching back and forth.

When you multitask, it is inevitable that each individual task will be slower and of lower quality, as you are going back and forth. Ask yourself why you are doing this activity. Is it to just mark it off the list or is it to get some result? Is your goal, in having a conversation with your friend, that you can say you talked to her this week or is it to actually listen to what she is saying and know that she has listened to you as well?

You simply cannot have quality while multitasking. You are not going to be productive if you multitask, as much as you may feel you are being productive. When caring for your parent and the rest of your life, every moment is going to count, and it is imperative that you have quality results, which will occur if you only perform one task at a time.

Not convinced? Fine. Humor me and try it for one day. Just for one day, do one single task at a time. No multitasking. Just do one task at a time. Just for one day. How did it feel? Were you able to do it? Were you able to actually enjoy your lunch today? Did you actually remember the conversation you had with a colleague or your child?

REMOVING OTHER DISTRACTIONS OR INTERRUPTIONS

After uni-tasking, I hope that you are convinced that you do a better job if you focus on one task at a time. Here is another incredibly powerful tool to help you keep your focus on the task at hand. Eliminate distractions and interruptions. This will be most useful at work so that when we are at work we are producing at a high level and getting results. Most of us have heard that it takes twenty-three minutes (or thereabout) for our brain to fully regain focus after an interruption or distraction. Yes, you might get back to your task or project, but your brain isn't 100 percent in yet.

I am not going to go into detail about how many distractions and stimuli we have in our world. I don't have the time. Suffice it to say that all of this new technology that is supposed to make our lives easier and give us more time not only hasn't, but it is causing us to be far less productive.

In order to really use any of the tools in this chapter, you are going to have to focus. You can't focus if you are getting alerts for every like, text, or email or checking to see if you got any likes, texts, or emails.

Step one is to cut the cord. Not entirely, but technology and your smartphone should work for you, not cause you to be a slave to an inanimate object. So, when you are driving, put the phone in the back seat. Not kidding. Not only may you save a life, but you can actually relax a bit in the car. Have a real conversation with one of your kids. There is nothing you need to do on your phone while you are driving. Really.

When caring for your parent, the time in your car may be the only quiet alone time you get that day. Enjoy that time and use it to calm your thoughts and relax a bit.

When you are at home, put your phone away. You are supposed to be with your family. They deserve your undivided attention. Likewise at work. This doesn't mean put your phone face down. It means turn off notifications and put it out of your line of sight.

There are plenty of distractions we can do nothing about. The dog is going to bark. The kids are going to come running through the house, and your assistant is just going to have to talk to you. However, there are a lot of things we can do to reduce the interruptions and distractions. The largest one is to silence your phone. Turn off notifications on everything. Silence your phone—not even on vibrate. Instruct your family to call your office in the event of an emergency. People were able to contact other people well before smartphones came along.

Close your office door and give strict instructions that no one is to knock or open that door. If there is bone or blood, then call 911, but no one interrupts you during the next ninety minutes—or whatever. If you have a big project and know how difficult it will be to do in peace, go to the library and get a private room to work in. I have known authors who have rented hotel rooms and taken the phone off the hook so they could write in peace. If the project is at home, hire a sitter to take the kids out for the day so that you can have the house to yourself for the day and really focus. Even just ninety minutes of real focus will produce results like you cannot imagine.

You control your time. There are plenty of other people out there who will steal it if you let them. Just think of the two scenarios below.

You have a work project that you are simply going to have to work on during the weekend. It should only take a few hours, and it is important.

Old Way

Procrastinate on Saturday, do errands, grocery shop, do laundry, transport kids to activities...and all of that time you are not focused on the activity at hand. You are not focused on your kids even though they are with you. You are still thinking about your project. It is haunting you. You are probably not as patient with your kids and don't really engage with them, as part of your brain is still thinking about your project.

You finally get to the project on Sunday afternoon. You are trying to work on it and feeling the pressure, as you know you have a limited time to do it. The freaking kids are not cooperating, nor do they care about your project. They are still playing, yelling, walking by and trying to talk to you, and your phone has rung a few times as well. You are either missing the game you wanted to watch, or you have it on, but on mute.

Your project is not getting done quickly and you know it is not great work. Then the next time someone runs through the house, or heaven forbid tries to talk to you, what do you do? You snap. "I told you I had work to do." Now you are upset. Your family is upset. And you still have this work to do. In your mindset, even if now your family is yelled into being quiet, what do you think your work product is going to be? Not your best.

You finally get it done and feel some relief. Now you have to go and try to do damage control with your family.

New Way

Friday evening, schedule your two hours of work time for Saturday morning, if possible. Tell your family about it and ask for their help so that you can get this work done. Explain to them how it is difficult to concentrate and focus, so that for two hours you are going to go to the library, office, home office, or whatever to work. Then go separate yourself so that you can do that. Turn off any way for people to reach you. Get your work done.

Given your focus, you will probably be done before the allotted two hours, and your work product will be a quality product. Now you are relaxed and can actually spend time with your family and be present with them on more than just a physical level. No yelling, no regrets, no drama, and no guilt.

You are also teaching others, through example, how to focus and concentrate, something younger generations are going to have to learn, given being raised with tablets, smartphones, and constant stimulation. Maybe they even do their own homework at the same time you are doing yours. Then the whole family can relax all weekend, knowing their most important tasks are done.

Prioritize and Limit Tasks

One is not going to get results or be productive without separating vital work from trivial work. This is the difference between being busy and really getting crap done and getting results. You are never going to be able to "get it all done." There is always something else that you could be doing. What counts and what is going to make the difference is getting the right things done; the important things done.

Once you get the vital things done, you can feel free to let the rest of the tasks go, knowing they don't really matter. You can do anything once you stop trying to do everything.

Ninety-Minute Jam Sessions

Ninety minutes is about as long as I, or most people, can really concentrate and focus before I need a break. So, I work in ninety-minute increments. This is especially helpful at work. For ninety minutes, I freakin' work. No calls, no appointments, no interruptions, no checking email, and no alerts. Just work. Then I take a ten- to fifteen-minute break and go back in for another ninety minutes. You would not believe what I am able to get accomplished even with one ninety-minute jam session a day, much less three or four.

I understand that if you are a physician, other medical

personnel, litigator, in sales, and so on, this model may not work for your day-to-day workday. However, when you are back in the office, the more you can employ this tactic, even if it isn't for ninety minutes, the more you will be amazed at the results.

So, depending on your work and life, you may need to tweak this model to fit your circumstances. The important thing is to do that and have uninterrupted time to really focus on your work every day.

Saying No

Your ability to produce results, and during this time stay sane, is going to largely also depend on your ability to say "no." I think, especially for women, we have not only not been taught to say "no," but we have been taught it is not nice to say "no." It is imperative to be able to be comfortable saying "no." Otherwise you become a martyr—overtaxed, overwhelmed, and people will steal your time.

During this time, and hopefully after, you are going to have to learn to say "no." "No" to new assignments that someone is asking you to do because they are lazy and don't want to do it. "No" to new or even existing volunteer "opportunities." "No" to that party you don't really want to go to. "No" to baking cupcakes for that event.

This can be difficult to do. Here is my lifesaving decision maker: if I can't instantly say "hell yes," then it is a "no." If I have any hesitation, resistance, "ahhh," then the answer is "no." I don't have time in my life for anything that is not a "hell yes." Every minute you are spending doing something that is not really important to you, you are taking that time away from what is important to you.

This leads me to your three main priorities.

THREE MAIN PRIORITIES

During any time in our lives, we should only really focus on three priorities at a time. More than that is just too much. These priorities change over time as life changes; however, all of our tasks should relate to our three priorities. If your number one most important task today is not related to your three main life goals, why is it a priority? This used to be one of my main life issues. I would have all of these goals, but my daily tasks were not related to them, or if tasks were on my to-do list, I wouldn't make them a priority. For instance, I would say that my health and losing weight were a top priority, and yet even if exercising got on the to-do list, I didn't make it a priority, and by the time I got to it, it was 7:00 p.m. and there was no way I was going to do it. I had nothing left. All of these other tasks had taken priority over the tasks that would have actually gotten me to the goals that I said were important to me.

Now my tasks are based on what my three main priorities are at any given time. The tasks that are not related to my three priorities either don't get done at all or they are done only when all other tasks have been completed. This tool really helped me be more disciplined and was a weekly and daily reminder of what my real priorities were.

So when caring for your parent, ask what your three main priorities are and base your actions on those three priorities.

Weekly Planning

Every week, I write out all of the things I need to do, should do, and want to do for the following week. I then use a chart with my three priorities on the chart as well as another category. Each of the items in my to-do list must fit into one of the categories. For instance, my current three categories are health (physical, emotional, spiritual); income and impact (firm and book); and continuing to simplify life as much as possible. These categories are what matter in my life now. As I was writing this book, my father's health declined, and he died. I had to shift my priorities a bit to give myself time to heal and rest. I also had to add handling his services and estate.

If one of your "to dos" doesn't fit into one of your three categories, it goes into the "other" category. I then really examine the "other" list. What can I hire someone else to take care of on the list? What can I delegate to my assistant to take care of for me? What can I just eliminate, as it is not a "hell yes"? Obviously, some things you just need to do yourself, such as going to the dentist.

I then go back to the three categories and start calendaring. It is important, actually vital, to calendar your tasks or else your calendar and day will fill up with items that are not priorities and not furthering your three main goals.

If having a better relationship or connection with your spouse or kids is one of your goals, then it needs to be on the list, and you need to have actual things to do each week to reach that goal. You are going to need to spend some time and energy to make those connections. So write in talking X number of hours to your spouse, spending X hours one-on-one with your child where you are connecting, or reading a book this week on relationships.

So my daily calendar is planned out so that I get what is important to my goals done every day. Then, if I have extra time, which I generally do as I haven't been wasting it, I can get to some of the "to dos" in the "other" category.

On your daily to-do list or calendar, do the hardest thing first. It isn't going to go away. It will haunt you the entire day. Just bite the bullet and get it done. Then the rest of the day is easy by comparison. We all know this, right? We all have had those tasks that we kept putting off, as we didn't want to do them. But then they just haunt us all day. Just do it and get it over with.

Now keep in mind that when caring for your parent, your entire day's plan or week's plan can go up in smoke at any moment. Know that ahead of time and be okay with that reality. Hopefully, with this plan you will have your most important tasks completed.

Bookend Your Day

Routines are good for us, in that they provide some structure, and we go into automatic pilot. That is, if the routine is good for us. Generally, when we first get up and right before we go to bed, we have the most control over our time.

Especially during this chaotic time, if you can take even half an hour in the morning and at the end of your day to ensure that you can at least stretch for a few minutes, journal, meditate, have an actual conversation with your spouse, take a walk, or sit and watch the sunrise with a cup of tea, it will do wonders for your life and help keep you centered. At least once or twice a day you can ensure that you are centered if you establish some healthy routines. Your day may have gone to shit, but you can go to bed feeling good and knowing that the dishes are washed, your face is clean, your teeth are brushed and flossed, and your mind is peaceful as you journal, read, or just relax. Whatever your morning and evening routine is, make it intentional. Just like an evening routine is good for your kids, it is good for you.

So, turn off all devices, TVs, and so on at least half an hour before going to bed, and do your nighttime routine. You will sleep far better. This is especially true when shit hits the fan and you may not even be sleeping at your home. I have had to fly across the country at a moment's notice at least four times in the recent years due to family health emergencies. I have literally had about ten minutes to pack and be on the road to an airport. I can't tell you what a difference it makes to have my bookends in place. Even when my schedule and routine have been thrown out the window, and I am sleeping in a hotel or hospital room, if I can have even most of my nighttime routine, I am okay. If I can even stretch for ten minutes in the morning and have my tea, I am okay. Ready for a day of chaos and total uncertainty.

OUTSOURCING

I used to have such a problem with the idea of hiring someone to help me do something I could do myself, especially when money was tight. I can do a lot of things myself. I knew my time should be valuable, but until I did the math, I really didn't understand or compute just how much.

What I didn't understand was that my time was worth a lot, even in the hours that I wasn't "earning" money. My "time off" was best used to do what I needed to do in order to refresh, revive, and enjoy life, so I could be fully ready to work and work well the next day. Every minute of every day was valuable.

You say you don't have the money to hire people? You might need to work harder to earn that extra few hundred dollars a month to pay for that housekeeper and then that will free up more time to make more money.

You say you're not comfortable with other people doing for you. Well, you can stay in your comfort zone or you can be a bit uncomfortable for a little bit and have more time and more money. Here are your two choices. You can either accept some help, get more done, and have a bit of peace, or you can continue on with how things are going.

Learn from my mistakes. When I was taking care of my mom, I didn't hire any help. I "didn't" have the money. Although, at that point, I had never even looked into what it would cost. I was cleaning my own home, my office, and my mother's apartment. Once a week I would go to her apartment, and instead of talking with her or spending quality time with her, I would hurry and clean her apartment. Her apartment was a small two-bedroom apartment and it would have probably cost me fifty dollars or less to have someone clean it. Even if I had help twice a month, it would have helped a lot. Yes, I had one hundred dollars that would have been far better spent on having my mom's apartment well cleaned and me working on my business or spending that time talking and having fun with my mother instead of cleaning her toilet.

So, what are some things that you could get some help with right now?

Some obvious ones are:

- Housekeeper
- Professional organizer/purger
- Gardener—even to just mow and trim the lawn
- Bookkeeper
- Grocery delivery
- Home projects: organizing, painting, decorating, or any repairs

HOW DO YOU EAT AN ELEPHANT?

One bite at a time. Caring for your parent is a huge

project. It can be completely overwhelming on its own, much less when thrown into your already full life. When one is faced with a large job, project, or task, it can be totally overwhelming.

What I find helps me is to break up the tasks into small, bite-size pieces. If you thought about eating an elephant (no, I don't want you to eat an elephant or hurt it in any way), it would be overwhelming. But, small bite by small bite, you could get it done, with enough time and consistency.

I used to use this technique when I ran. I don't like running. Before I started training for my first marathon, I could not run a mile. Seriously. I have disliked every step when I have run. Yet I have completed two marathons, which entails a lot of training, a lot of miles, and a hell of a lot of steps. When things got tough out on the road, I would pick a spot in the road or trail fairly close to me and tell myself—just get past that. Just get past that mailbox, line, tree—whatever. Then I would pick another spot—again pretty close to me, as in no more than two hundred feet and sometimes less than ten. Sometimes I would stop and rest when I reached my spot, but most of the time, I would keep on going. These little goals kept me moving—one foot in front of the other.

When I began this book, my publisher and friend, Tucker,

gave me the task of writing 250 words on my writing days. That is essentially a paragraph. Even on my absolute worst day, when I would rather put acid in my eye than write, I can do 250 words. Why did Tucker give me such a low number? Because he knows that no one can write just 250 words. You really just can't. Your fingers just keep typing or your hand just keeps writing on the paper. So, even when you know you can stop, you don't. I generally write two to three pages a day. Yet if that were my daily goal, I would have a difficult time getting myself to sit down and start every day. It would be too daunting.

So, you are now facing a huge project with no firm end date and totally unknown new experiences ahead of you. It will be important to use this tool and break up this project as much as possible into small bites. Set small goals each day—sometimes you might need to set a goal so small it is just for thirty minutes. Just get through the next thirty minutes.

All you have to do right now is get Mom to the doctor, or whatever the task may be. Work on that and only that, without thinking of the big picture or even your next step. One step at a time. One bite at a time. That is all. You don't have to convince yourself to do everything, just the next thing.

You are in, or will be in, survival mode, and these tools

will prove to be of great use to you during this time. And if you continue to use these tools, even after this time, and in all areas of your life, you will be amazed at how much you can get done. You will actually get results in the important things in your life.

Had I had these tools when my mother was ill and dying, and after she died, my world would have been far easier, and the damage far less than it was. But one has to use these tools consistently. Just like walking twenty minutes a few times a year is not going to do anything for your health, using these tools intermittently is not going to do anything to help you manage your time yourself.

So, what are your time thieves? What activities are you allowing to steal your time? What people do you allow to steal your time? What tasks can you immediately get off of your plate? What can you say "no" to? What tasks can you outsource? What big tasks can you break into small pieces?

What are your six priorities today? What one thing is going to have the largest impact? What one thing will matter in a year from now if you do or don't do it?

Chapter Six

SELF-CARE

---

*Self-care is giving the world the best of
you, instead of what's left of you.*

—KATIE REED

This chapter will focus on dealing with your own life during this stressful time. Specifically, your own needs, your career, marriage, friends, and children. Flight attendants instruct us that, in the case of an emergency, we should put our own oxygen mask on first before trying to help anyone else. If you don't, you won't have the oxygen needed to help that other person, and then you both go down.

So we are going to start with taking care of yourself. You can't give what you don't have. We all have some of the same basic needs, such as shelter, safety, food, water, sleep, and minimal resources. Each one of us also has our own individual needs that differ from one another that are just as important to attend to as food, water, and shelter.

BASIC NEEDS

I understand that this seems ridiculously elementary. I also understand that during periods of great stress and being in survival mode, it is easy to neglect your most basic needs. This will only further our stress and negative consequences. So, at the risk of treating you like a five-year-old, here we go.

- Water. It is easy, on a regular day, to neglect to drink water on a regular basis. Every single function in your body and mind requires water. There is nothing more important to life. Basic life and death stuff here, people. Keep a water bottle with you and drink eight glasses a day. Even if you need to set an alarm to remind yourself to do it.
- Food. When was the last time you ate anything? That is a question that is asked of many a caregiver or someone holding a vigil over a loved one. Many people in this situation just don't eat. They don't feel hungry, and they simply don't eat. Others overeat comfort food. Now is not the time to spend energy you don't have going on that new diet or completely changing your lifestyle, but it is essential that you eat regularly, at least twice a day and preferably three, and that you

have at least some nutrients in your food. I can also tell you that hospital cafeterias have some of the worst food for your body. It is ridiculous. So stock up on vegetables, fruits, and nuts that are easy to transport. The first time my father got really ill, my dear friend drove me to the airport and handed me a bag full of nuts and other healthy snacks. It was a lifesaver. Not only for me, but my brothers as well. Without it, we would have eaten crap food from vending machines, which would have made us feel worse than we did. I am not going to go into what you should or shouldn't eat, as I am assuming you know that information or can easily find out. What I will say is that eating processed food, chips, candy, sweets, and a lot of empty calories will only make you feel worse, and you can't afford that right now.

· Sleep. As difficult as it may be at times, it is imperative that you get sufficient sleep, which means eight to nine hours. Given all of the scientific evidence, I hope that most people have been convinced that sleep doesn't make you a weak person; just the opposite. No one is high functioning when they lack sleep. Not going to argue about it. Get sleep every night. Even if it means taking a Benadryl. Do what needs to be done so you can have at least a chance of a good night's sleep by having good sleep hygiene. TV and other electronics off half an hour before bed, no alcohol a few hours before going to sleep, take a warm bath, read, journal, whatever it takes to get your mind prepared to go to sleep.

- Exercise. I hate to exercise. I really do. Yet, my body, mind, and mental health all need exercise. So, during this time, even if it means just doing some stretching every day, even in a hospital room, or walking the corridor of the assisted living facility a few times—get some exercise in every day.

YOUR UNIQUE NEEDS, YOUR SOUL FOOD

In addition to the common needs above, each of us has our own needs that differ from every other person alive. They are what make us unique. They need to be met, even to a minimal degree, for us to be content, much less happy. They are what feeds your soul. When we have enough, we feel grounded, centered, and ourselves. And when we don't have enough of even one, we feel off, uncentered, anxious, and unhappy. It can take work to even recognize what your individual needs are, much less meet them. Make no mistake, though, if these needs are not met in some way, you will continually be off-center. Some are greater than others and need more attention. Others we can meet every now and again and be fine.

The best way to explain these needs is to give you the example of my soul food.

It includes:

- Structure
- Excellence
- Health
- Financial health—paying bills with ease and living how I want to live
- Family/friends
- Achievement
- Creativity
- Beauty
- Travel
- Intellectual stimulation and learning
- Home
- Solitude
- Simplicity
- Impact

I won't go into each of these, but I'll explain a few to give you an idea of what I mean by my soul food.

I need structure in my life. I need a schedule even when I work at home. I want to know what is coming up next and how long it should take. I am not a fly-by-the-seat-of-my-pants girl. Not having structure makes me very anxious and unhappy. I just do better with structure.

So, during the really stressful times of life, such as caring for a sick loved one, it is even more important for me to have some structure in my life to keep me grounded and feeling like myself. I am never going to be that person who wakes up and is okay staying in pajamas all day and having absolutely no plan for the day. So I need this soul food every single day.

One soul food I don't need every day is creativity. I like to think I am a fairly creative person. I need a certain level of creativity in my life. However, that doesn't mean that I need to take photos, decorate, or paint every day, every week, or even every month. However, if it has been "too long" since I have done something creative, I do start to itch, and that itching only gets stronger until I release it by doing something creative. So, every few months I take an art class or take three to four hours and go take some photos, and at least every week I need to think about writing, workshops, or other creative outlets and at least write notes in journals.

My home is very important to me and always has been. I don't need a terribly valuable home filled with expensive treasures. I do need a clean home that is free from clutter and is decorated nicely. Even during my poorest period in life, when my son and I lived on eighty dollars per month for food, I went to the dollar store, purchased sheets, and made curtains for our apartment. If my home is a mess, then that means everything in my life has gone to shit, as that is my last safety net for my mental health. So, no matter what is going on in my life, my home needs to have some order and cleanliness.

Before you just start listing things, I would suggest that you take at least an hour or two to be by yourself in a quiet space so that you can really feel and think. Close your eyes and ask yourself what you really need to be content. What is your soul food? Don't make judgments about it either. Your soul food is your soul food.

What do you need and what does it mean to need it? Do you need a bit of solitude every day or week? What does that mean? How much do you need to be satisfied? An hour alone every day? Every week? Five hours every day?

I would also think about the range of what is the absolute minimum you need of this item in your life. Especially during this stressful time. Say creativity is on your soul food list. You might not be able to take the time to take that four-hour painting class, but maybe you can sketch for even ten minutes a day. Hell, sing in the car. The important thing is to recognize what your soul needs and to feed it what it needs.

I have a cousin, Chris, who has few soul food needs. Far fewer than mine. One of his is to be in nature—specifically, hiking and sleeping outdoors. This soul food need of his is huge. He needs a lot of it to function, much less be happy. Rain, shine, snow, or sun he needs to hike. He needs it every week. Period. I would really not want to be around this man if he hadn't been able to go on a good hike for a month.

I have another friend, Jennifer, who has a soul food need of feeling needed. She has to feel needed on a regular basis. At times, this need has gotten her into some trouble, but she has learned to monitor it and rein it in. However, that soul food need remains. It is just part of who she is and what makes her tick.

The more you know yourself and your needs, the more content you will be, especially if you are vigilant about meeting those needs. So, what is your soul food and how much of it do you need?

Keep that in mind during this time. When you really start to get irritated, anxious, depressed, and so on, think about what soul foods you are starving for and go feed on them—even a little bit.

Taking care of yourself is not optional. You can't take care of the other people you need to take care of without taking care of yourself first. So yes, this really does need to be a top priority, if not the top priority.

I also want to note that there is a difference between taking care of oneself and self-indulgence. It took me many years to recognize this, and I only did so after a friend pointed it out to me. Taking care of myself means being kind to myself, eating what my body needs to function well, exercising, getting enough sleep, and so on. Taking care of myself doesn't mean spending money I don't have, neglecting important tasks to watch Netflix all day, or eating cupcakes because "I deserve them." It took me a while to get this concept. So I started asking myself how I would take care of a child. I would make sure that child got sleep, good food, and downtime. I wouldn't allow them to eat two cupcakes, much less say they "deserved" them. I know that indulging a child is not good for that child. Neither is it good for us.

MARRIAGE

When I say marriage, I am including any intimate relationship, regardless of the title. I am not going to say much about this, other than to say that quality over quantity is going to be important during this time. You may not have the time or energy for a romantic weekend getaway, but you do have time for a hug and a heartfelt "thank you." Your partner is an adult and is fully able to care for him or herself. You don't need to care for your partner. You do need to pay some attention to the relationship. Even if you aren't spending a lot of time on the relationship, little gestures will go a long way.

It is going to be important for you to tell your partner what you need and want from him or her. Do not expect him to be able to read your mind or intuitively know what you need. That isn't fair. If you need him to be more vigilant about tidying up, then say so. If you need more physical affection or less, then say so. I see a lot of people, mostly women, expecting their partner to "know" what they need. Hell, most of the time *you* don't know what you need, yet you are expecting your partner to know? Also, be as specific as possible. "I need you to do more around the house" doesn't mean anything. "I need you to do the dishes every day" does. Also, doing the dishes means putting them away.

The other thing that I would say about relationships during this time is to pay attention. Stressful times like this can make or break a relationship. How your partner handles this stress is really something to pay attention to, as it tells you a lot about him or her. Does she step up to the plate and do extra things without being asked? Does he ask you what you need from him? Is his immediate response to put your needs first or his? When he knows you have had a fourteen-hour day, haven't eaten, and are beyond exhausted, does he still want to have sex? What does that tell you? Does your spouse have to make a big deal when he does do something without being asked?

I am not suggesting that you freak out, file for divorce, or make any major changes to the relationship. That is the last thing you need during this time. What I am suggesting is that you make mental notes about his or her ability to handle life's storms. Is your partner showing support through behavior or just words? Is the pattern putting your needs first or expecting things to be status quo? Just pay attention.

KIDS

You may very well have younger children at the same time in which you are caring for a dying parent. It can be difficult to know how much to tell them and how much to involve them, as you want to protect them from as much pain as possible. Clearly, your parenting decisions are up to you, but I do have some opinions. I myself was a young child when my grandmother and my aunt, both of whom lived with us, died. I have a unique perspective given that I have lived through these experiences as a child.

The first thing I would say is that you should give your child(ren) some credit. They know and understand a whole lot more than most people acknowledge. If there is some big secret going on in the house, whispered conversations behind closed doors, and you are suddenly short-tempered or crying, they clearly know something bad is happening. If you don't share what it is, their imaginations are going to fill in the blanks. What they imagine is probably going to be worse than the reality. Not knowing is going to cause more harm in that what they imagine may cause more trauma to them. Their brain doesn't know if what they are imagining is real or not—the trauma is the same.

Likewise, I wouldn't suggest making this "no big deal" either. It is a big deal. They are going to be facing a lot of pain when they lose someone they love, and they need to be prepared for that. I remember clearly the time period when my aunt Betty died. She had lived with us for five years and had helped raise me. I loved her very much. Suddenly, she was in the hospital, and the only information I got was that she was really sick. I was eight. I didn't understand that she could actually die, much less that she was on death's door. I saw her one time in the hospital, and I acted like it was no big deal. Then, all of a sudden, she was dead. It was a big surprise to me. I never got to really say goodbye to her or tell her I loved her one last time.

I know my mother was trying to shield me from pain. However, ultimately, it didn't shield me, and I was completely unprepared for the pain I felt and had no way of knowing how to cope with it. I don't know what, if anything, I would have done differently at eight, but it would have been nice to have known more information—age appropriate, obviously.

Your kids can feel something isn't right. Consider their age, but please tell them what is going on so they can begin to process it. Death is a part of life and they should understand this fact. This also gives you some time to help them deal with things while you are not in the deepest depths of your own grief when your parent actually dies.

I would also recommend that you involve them in some way in what you are doing to care for your parent. This may seem a bit shocking to you, but hear me out. Your kids probably want to feel included in this family project. They want to help. They love their grandparents, hopefully. This is a great learning and bonding opportunity for the entire family, and specifically for your kids with their grandparent. Please do not take that away from your child in an attempt to shield them from this "horrible" event.

What does involving them look like? It depends on the child and their age. I am not suggesting that you have a child taking physical care of their grandparent. But there are a lot of ways in which they can contribute and feel good about helping someone they love. I still smile and feel great when I read my mother's journals about me growing up with my grandmother. My grandmother was in her eighties and died when I was almost three. My mother's journals are filled with story after story about my interactions with my grandmother. Even as an infant and toddler I gave my grandmother much joy and laughter until the day she died. I don't remember my grandmother, but I know in my soul we were connected, and I gave her as much as she gave me. I made an old lady very happy and filled her life with laughter the last two years of her life. That feels pretty great.

So, what can your child do? They can help out around the house. Explain how that extra bit of work is really helping you so that you can help Grandma. They can sit with, read to, and play games with their grandparent, freeing up some time for you to do other things. If they are old enough to drive, they can do errands or help with some of the extra transportation duties. When my mother died, my oldest son spent the night with her a few times so I could get a good night's sleep. It was good for her and good for him. I am so glad he had that special time with his grandmother. My youngest two boys would visit my mother. Her mind had started to go. She didn't recognize them but talked about how wonderful it was that the Boy Scouts stopped by. My youngest was only nine at the time, but he completely rolled with it and didn't act surprised or question her weird statement. They brought her joy, and I think it was good for them to see and spend time with her even if she didn't recognize them. Ask your kids how they would like to contribute to their grandparent's care.

Regardless of what is going on in your life or your aging or dying parent's life, your kids still need a bath tonight. You probably also want to make sure that your kids have consistency and their routine is as static as possible. However, given your extra responsibilities, that may not always be possible. You and they may have to make some choices in whether they are able to do all of the extracurricular activities they usually do, and so on. I would urge you to involve them in those decisions. Maybe for just a little while they have one or two extracurricular activities, not four or five?

You are going to have to decide, preferably with your child, what extra activities are most important. For instance, maybe this holiday season you do only a few holiday outings. Ask them what is most important to them. My then-husband's father died December 6. My mother died on December 10. Not kidding. I don't remember much of that Christmas—or really any of it—but I know that we still put up a Christmas tree and decorations. There was no getting around that everyone's Christmas was ruined, but traditions are important for everyone and tend to ground us a bit. It was really painful, especially getting her Christmas ornaments on the tree, but I think it would have been worse if we hadn't.

My father died on December 13th, 2018. Not sure what my parents have against December. In any event, I put up my Christmas decor, and it was grounding for me. Yes, it was painful to put up his stocking, but it was important to do so.

Remember that your kids are learning from you every second of every day. They will not learn much from what you tell them but will learn a great deal from how you behave. When you are behaving as a martyr, that is how they will learn to behave. When you are short tempered because you are under stress, that is how they will behave when they are under stress. When you don't take care of your needs, they won't take care of theirs when they are adults either. So treat yourself as you would like your children to treat themselves when they are adults.

WORK

Regardless of whether you own your own business and have some flexibility in scheduling how many hours you work each week, or whether you work for someone else and have little to no flexibility, we all have responsibilities to others and generally can't just take time off work to care for our parents.

There are no easy solutions to the work issue. There is generally no time frame that you can give to your employer either. There are some tools that you can use to get through caring for your parents and still have a job, business, or career at the end of that period.

The first is clear communication to your clients, boss, and coworkers about what is going on and what that means for them. Regardless of what kind of people you work for, at the end of the day, everyone is selfish and wants to know how they are going to be affected by your absence in person or in mind.

Really try to plan out what time you can take off so that you can use that time wisely and hopefully at a time that will least damage the workplace. Think through what a reasonable time is to take off and when. This will save you from making emotional decisions later on that are not as effective as possible.

We can all only take off so much time, so let's use that time to its maximum effect. For instance, arrange other transport to and from doctors' appointments and talk to your parent's doctor on the phone. If your parent is in the hospital a lot, then maybe only take time off at X point. For instance, several times, I dropped everything to travel across the country when my father was ill. I am glad I did all three times. However, I couldn't do that indefinitely.

When my grandma Wolden was diagnosed with cancer, and hospice was called in, I knew that I could only really afford to go to see her once. I could go see her when she was still able to communicate, or to her funeral, but not both. The decision was easy, and I went to see her while she could still talk with me, hold my hand, and tell me she loved me. When she passed away, it did feel a bit odd not to attend her funeral, but I knew that I had made the correct decision and spent that time wisely.

While you are at work, use your time/self-management tools and do a freaking great job when you are there. When you are at work, work. Get shit done. When you are not at work, don't think twice about it. If you are doing quality work and getting results, then your clients, coworkers, or boss should be patient with you. One can hope.

If you are going to need more time and can afford it, consider taking family leave if you qualify. Your job will be protected, and you can concentrate on caring for your loved one.

Now is probably not the time to try to push for that promotion, take on a lot of extra responsibilities at work, or try that new marketing program. You are likely not going to have the extra time, energy, or brainpower that you need to take on that new "opportunity." It, or something like it, will be there when you are at 100 percent, I swear.

LIFE WILL BE DIFFERENT WITH SOME SELF-CARE

A stressful time can feel very isolating, like you are the only person who has or is going through something like this. You are not. You are also not the only person in the picture who is struggling. Be patient with yourself and be patient with others around you. When your kids start acting out or your parent is snappy, remember that everyone touched by this situation is hurting, tired, scared, and grieving. Everyone just needs a little bit more kindness, including you.

As I was writing this chapter, my father went into the hospital again, then ICU, and then died. Again, this was days after closing on the sale of my home and moving into an apartment. Had it not been for what I had learned, and am now sharing with you, about keeping my shit together, I would have either been in the fetal position in bed, unable to move, or I would have been racing around like a chicken with its head cut off, getting nothing accomplished in a frenzied panic. Don't get me wrong; it was not a pleasant time in my life, and I did lose my shit a few times. But for an hour, not days, weeks, or months.

I had the tools to get through it. And although I needed to concentrate a lot more on what the tools were and how to use them, I did use them. I was able to plan ahead and call my realtor to see if I could sign early so that if I needed to leave for Montana, I could. I was able to rationally decide that there was no point in me immediately going up to Montana when my dad was sedated, and it would be far better for me to stay in Texas and get the move done so that I had a home to live in, no matter what happened in the next week or month.

Now, to be clear, the evening I moved into my apartment I had toast, red wine, and half of a good chocolate bar for dinner and watched too much Netflix while talking to family members. So much for no self-indulgence. I cried myself to sleep and then was up several times during the night. The next morning, I felt like a Mack truck had hit me. However, my head was clear. I was able to think about what I had to accomplish and what I needed to do in order to take care of myself. Every decision had to have maximum impact, or I didn't do it. I didn't take on too much.

As a result, this go-around with my father (as opposed to when my mother was ill and died) was just completely better. I was much calmer, took care of myself, and was able to take better care of him. With my mom, I was a complete mess probably 70 to 80 percent of the time during the last month of her life. With my dad, it was maybe 5 percent. I attribute most of that success to me taking my own advice, using my time tools, and taking care of myself. I was also far better able to cope when my dad died.

Use your time tools, do what is vital, and let the rest go. Answer these questions now. In times of stress, come back to these guidelines.

1. What are your guidelines for taking care of yourself? What is your soul food and how much of it do you need to function? It is really important to think this through ahead of time so that when shit really hits the fan, you can stop yourself from losing it and go to your list: "Okay, I need to eat, take a walk, go be by myself for an hour, get a message, take a nap—whatever." Above all, be kind to yourself.

2. What will you do to nurture your relationship/marriage during this time? On a daily basis, weekly, monthly?

3. What will you discuss with the kids? Can you come up with some specifics so that you don't forget what is important during an emotional discussion?

4. How will you involve your kids in any care for the family?

5. How will you establish and keep boundaries with other people without losing your temper or backing down and taking on more than you want? Remember, "No thank you" is a full sentence. There is no need to offer an explanation. Your time and energy are a higher priority than not wanting to hurt someone's feelings or wanting to go along with someone else's plan. Remember, if it isn't a "hell yes," that is, your instincts say it is a yes, then it is a no.

6. Above all else, be kind and gentle with yourself.

Chapter Seven

ELDER ABUSE

Power is no blessing in itself, except when it is used to protect the innocent.
—JONATHAN SWIFT

He just had to make it to 5:00 p.m. Twenty minutes; he could do it. Seventeen minutes. He could do this. Twelve minutes and she would be gone, until the next shift in the morning. He had lived through this before and he was damn sure going to live through it again. The first time he was twelve and in Auschwitz. Now, he was eighty-eight and in Shady Court Assisted Living Home.

This chapter is short and ugly. It is absolutely necessary that you have even an elementary knowledge of the signs and symptoms of elder abuse and take some steps to prevent the same. According to the National Center on Elder Abuse, one out of every ten elderly Americans is abused before they die. And that is the abuse that is reported.

It is widely accepted that elder abuse is underreported due to shame, embarrassment, fear, or not being able to communicate.

Elder abuse takes many forms, ranging from neglect to physical abuse, sexual abuse, verbal abuse, emotional abuse, and financial abuse. No one is immune. One of the most famous cases of elder abuse was the New York socialite Brooke Astor. Her inner circle included friends such as Henry and Nancy Kissinger, David Rockefeller, Liz Smith, and Annette de la Renta. Even with all of her money and powerful friends, she still was terribly abused and neglected by her son and daughter-in-law. It took a lot of work from her grandson and her very rich and powerful friends to get her out of a horrible situation. If it can happen to Brooke Astor, it can happen to anyone.

Elder abuse doesn't have to be so dramatic. I knew an elderly woman, Claire, who had some significant funds. Her daughter was caring for her and did ensure that her mother's basic needs were met. However, it was clear that, in decision after decision, her daughter made cost cutting (in order to save her inheritance) the utmost priority. The mother had lived a lovely lifestyle until her daughter was in charge. Then she was moved to a safe, albeit plain, home that was nothing like her former facility. The cost was $8,000 less per month, though. The mother could not have outspent her money. She should have lived out the rest of her days in a beautiful facility where she was comfortable. Instead, she spent her last two months in a small, dark, depressing room in a cheap facility so that her daughter would have a larger inheritance. I did attempt to remedy the situation but was not legally able to take any action, as there was no "actual" abuse, neglect, or a crime going on. To this day, I get furious when I think of how she was treated.

The elderly or ill are especially susceptible to abuse, as many times they are isolated or unable to communicate. Some have memory problems that make it next to impossible to get credible statements from them. They certainly can't fight back. Predators understand this fact. Adding to the issue, many healthcare workers are poorly trained, poorly paid, and not treated well themselves. Their job is not a great job. They have to put up with a lot, do jobs most wouldn't want to do, and are paid next to nothing. While the vast majority of caregivers do a great job and care about their patients, many don't. They also know that the chances of them ever getting caught are slim to none. In late 2018, a woman in Arizona who had been in a coma for a long time was found to be pregnant. There are sick people out there who have no problem abusing people—even raping a woman in a coma.

Here are the types of abuse most common among the elderly, or other adults who are not able to communicate well, along with what to keep an eye on in order to identify if abuse is going on.

FINANCIAL ABUSE

Financial abuse occurs when money or belongings are stolen, or someone is manipulated or pressured to give money or buy items. It can also be "borrowing" money with no real intent of paying it back. It can include forging checks, taking someone's retirement and Social Security benefits, or using another's credit cards and bank accounts. It includes changing names on estate-planning documents, bank accounts, life insurance policies, or the title to a home. It can also include not keeping the person's standard of living to the historical standard of living when there are funds to do so, in an attempt to "save" money so there is more to inherit.

I have listed this first, as I believe it is the most prevalent abuse facing incapacitated or otherwise vulnerable adults. It is also rarely reported. I know that in my own family, a certain member has stolen from various relatives at least seven different times, yet the authorities have never been called. Family members are reluctant to call the police on other family members, and so the cycle continues.

Financial abuse is also difficult to prosecute, as family

members are reluctant to cooperate or simply don't remember what occurred.

Signs

- Withdrawals from bank accounts that your loved one can't explain
- A new "friend" who is getting too close, too fast
- Legal documents have been changed or have disappeared
- Missing financial statements
- Increased bills for normal expenses such as food, clothing, or odd purchases
- Signatures that seem to be forged
- Unpaid bills, utilities that are shut off, or threats of eviction

As a side note, bank tellers are trained in the signs of financial abuse in the elderly. They are many times the first line of defense against such abuse. If you have your parent's power of attorney, don't be surprised if they make it difficult for you to withdraw large sums of money. It is easy to get offended and frustrated. Just remember why they are giving you a hard time.

EMOTIONAL ABUSE

Sometimes called psychological abuse, this can include

a caregiver saying hurtful words, yelling, threatening, or repeatedly ignoring the person. It can be playing games by threatening to withhold medication, food, or other essentials. It also includes isolating the person and keeping the person from seeing close friends or relatives. Essentially, it is the caregiver being mean.

Signs

- Acting withdrawn or frightened
- Changes in their behavior that you can't explain
- Rocking back and forth or mumbling to themselves
- Being depressed, confused, or losing interest in things he or she enjoyed
- Having trouble sleeping
- Acting agitated
- Not taking part in activities he or she enjoys   .

NEGLECT

Neglect is when the caregiver does not try to respond to the person's needs.

Signs

- Person is messy or unclean. May have dirty clothing, unkempt hair or nails, or skin rashes
- Loses weight quickly or isn't hungry anymore

- Has bedsores
- Has missing or broken dentures, eyeglasses, hearing aids, or other medical devices

PHYSICAL ABUSE

This occurs when someone causes bodily harm, including, but not limited to, hitting, pushing, pinching, or slapping.

Signs

- Unexplained burns, cuts, bruises, or bleeding, or just far too many of them
- Sprained or broken bones
- Injuries that happen over and over
- The person doesn't want to see a doctor about his or her wounds
- Signs from the emotional abuse section

SEXUAL ABUSE

Sexual abuse involves a caregiver forcing an older adult, or any other non-consenting adult, to watch or be part of sexual acts. This can include what would be classified as sexual harassment as well. It doesn't just mean rape.

Signs

- Torn or bloody clothing, especially underwear
- A sexually transmitted disease
- Bruises, especially on both sides of the body or around the breasts or genitals
- Bleeding from the vagina or bottom.
- Signs from the emotional abuse section
- Pregnancy

WHAT TO DO IF YOU SUSPECT ANY ABUSE OR NEGLECT

First of all, don't discount your gut senses. If you feel something is "off," don't rationalize it away. Trust your gut. Even if you don't see signs specifically listed above. You know your parent. You know if they are acting like they don't want to be around a specific person, if they would never buy X, or if something else is amiss.

Depending on the severity, I don't recommend immediately talking to your parent about your suspicions. I disagree with some others on this, as I think it is too easy for the victim to deny what is going on, and then you are left with nothing. Obviously, this depends on the severity of what you suspect and the evidence you have.

If you think you have some time, do a bit of investigation. Set up nanny cams to video what is going on. Maybe hire a forensic accountant to check the books. Change caregivers and see if things improve. I say this because an abuser is an abuser, and if she is not caught and prosecuted, she will just go on to her next victim. I believe you have a duty to at least attempt to prevent that from happening to someone else.

Once you have some evidence, or it is reasonably clear that you are not going to get any, then take the action necessary to prevent further harm, and remove the perpetrator or suspected perpetrator from their victim. Call the police. Call Adult Protective Services. Get a restraining order or other protective order. Do what you need to do to protect your person.

We all have a duty to keep an eye on any elderly person or otherwise vulnerable adult we have contact with. Whether that be a neighbor or another resident in a home or hospital, it isn't going to hurt to keep an eye out for anything that seems odd or concerning. There are many people in nursing homes or assisted living homes who literally have no one. *No one* is visiting them or watching out for them. I am not saying violate boundaries or privacy, but if you see something odd, don't discount it. Ask questions. Just like if you saw a young child walking on a sidewalk by herself, you wouldn't just walk by. Neither should you just walk by a vulnerable adult who has clear signs of neglect or abuse.

Who Are These Monsters?

Most are just like you and me. There are some who are true monsters, with absolutely no morals or conscience and no remorse about anything they do. However, there are also the "normal" people who are stressed out, don't have the skills to handle such stress, and lash out. They are the people who are able to justify in their own mind that, somehow, they are entitled to "the money." That what they are doing isn't really that bad.

Early on in my legal career, I defended a woman, Molly, who had been accused of stealing from an elderly and incompetent woman she was supposed to be caring for. Molly seemed to be a caring individual who had no criminal history. I think she truly cared for this woman and continued to be hurt and shocked that she would never be able to see her again. She never admitted the theft, although she did enter a plea admitting that there was sufficient evidence against her to find her guilty. She had started out as a paid caregiver. The elderly woman's family was not very involved with her (clearly). Molly had stopped being paid as a caregiver but had stayed on. There was never an allegation that she didn't take great physical and emotional care of her client. The allegation was that she started stealing by just adding some things for herself into the grocery cart that not were meant for her client and for which her client paid. By the end, she had, allegedly, had her client sign a full power of attorney naming my client, as well as sign a quit claim deed to my client for her house, which was owned outright.

The police were notified by a bank teller after my client had withdrawn all funds from the elderly woman's bank accounts. The elderly woman was completely incompetent. She couldn't even tell the detectives her name.

Clearly, this was alleged theft on a grand scale and from the most vulnerable person one could imagine. I really think that Molly believed that somehow it wasn't theft, as she continued to care for the elderly woman, her family didn't care about her, and she was going to die soon anyway, so why shouldn't she get it instead of the woman's uncaring family?

If you met her, you wouldn't think she was a monster. You would think she was a kind and nurturing person. If you didn't know this story, you would have had no reason not to trust her to care for a vulnerable adult.

Any sort of elder abuse can happen to any elderly person or vulnerable adult. They are completely defenseless. All of us, but especially those of us with parents in this category, must learn to recognize the signs of any sort of abuse to the point where we could smell it a mile away.

Take a few minutes and think about a plan to protect your

loved one. What is your safety net? Are there sufficient people monitoring things so that anything odd would be detected quickly? How well do you know your parent's caregivers? How difficult would it be for someone to abuse or take advantage of your parent? If you don't have a strong safety net, what can you do to improve it?

For more information about elder abuse and where to get help:

National Center on Elder Abuse

1-855-500-3537
https://ncea.acl.gov

National Adult Protection Services Association

1-217-523-4431
www.napsa-now.org

National Domestic Violence Hotline

1-800-799-7233
www.thehotline.org/get-help

Chapter Eight

OTHERS

How people treat you is their Karma.
How you respond is yours.

—WAYNE DYER

I was in court, having presented a motion to continue a routine hearing in a misdemeanor criminal case, when the prosecutor said this to the judge: "I object to any further continuances of this matter, Your Honor. Ms. Long indicated that her mother would die last week. What guarantee do we have that her mother will actually die this week?"

Most people that you come into contact with will be momentarily kind, ask you how you are doing, ask if there is anything they can do, and so on. This kindness doesn't last long, frankly. Then there are others who are just assholes. People are inherently impatient, selfish, and self-interested. They will give you a bit of leeway until it starts to affect them and their lives. Don't take it personally. But also don't expect people to go out of their way to be kind to you or give you a break in any way. If you do, you will be disappointed. Especially if this situation goes on for over a week or two.

SIBLINGS

I grew up an only child, but when I found my biological family, I discovered I have three sets of siblings from my biological parents. I am close to my three brothers on my father's side. Luckily, my brothers and I really get along. They are incredible people.

In my practice, I have dealt with many sibling issues within families. It turns out that birth order really is a thing, with the oldest child or children, regardless of their abilities, many times believing they are or should be in charge. When a younger sibling has the power of attorney or takes the leadership role, it can cause issues within the family. I once represented the extremely capable adult daughter in a dispute with her two older sisters. My client, Jan, was doing a great job caring for her father, and there was no actual accusation of any malfeasance on her part. The two older sisters, one of whom was thought to be mentally ill, just didn't like the fact that their father had put their younger sister in charge. They went so far as to try to trick their father into signing over his power of attorney to them. What it came down to was that they had just gotten their noses out of joint and wanted to be in charge.

In any group, including families, one person usually emerges as the leader. (You can guess who that is in my family.) If you are the leader, then you have the responsibility to be a good leader, not push your own agenda on your siblings or tell them what is going to happen. Nothing good comes from that. Lead by example. Always take their thoughts and feelings into consideration and establish healthy boundaries when necessary.

Unfortunately, in some families the dynamics may necessitate establishing boundaries to protect your parent as well. This can still be done with love and kindness. Now *is not* the time or the place to bring up or hash out old shit. It simply has no place here.

In any family, there are usually one or two siblings who do most of the heavy lifting. They are the ones who are taking care of the logistics and transportation, talking with doctors, and doing the work of taking care of the parent. Most of the time this isn't "fair." Guess what? Life isn't fair. If you are the sibling doing all of the work, then I have a few suggestions. First, recognize that it might actually be simpler and easier to not have more cooks in the kitchen. Do you really want all of your siblings each calling the doctor for information or trying to coordinate who will drive Dad where and when? You could be creating a bloody mess by spreading the workload.

If there is something that you think a sibling would be good at doing and will actually help you, then ask. Maybe he can come and stay with your parent for a week to give you a break? Maybe she can be in charge of one thing. There is a fine line between being a martyr and having too many cooks in the kitchen and nothing getting accomplished.

I do think it is reasonable to insist that if someone takes on X job, they do it and do a good job, or do not take it on. Otherwise, their poor job will only create more chaos. So ask for a true commitment, and if they screw it up, then they don't get the privilege of doing more.

I was alone when taking care of my mother. With my father, my youngest brother and I took the lead in his care, with my brother doing most of the heaving lifting, as he was physically with my father. We work really well together and bonded in a way we never would have without going through this together.

I know another woman whose family coordinated scheduling her care. People who were able to work from home went and cared for her, for months at a time, and then another family member would take over for a few months. It was really beautiful to see this family working together.

Your siblings will stay in your life long after your parent leaves. How you and your siblings behave and treat each other during this time can be the difference between a family staying together and never speaking to one another again. Seriously.

You can no more control your siblings, nor should you, than you have ever been able to. You can control how you respond to any of their actions or lack of action. Try to not be too judgmental. Come with the love.

YOUR KIDS

Regardless of their age, your kids feel your stress, depression, and anxiety. They are also going through their own grief. So be patient, and don't freak out if they freak out. Also, don't be surprised if there is a lack of visible emotion. That doesn't mean that your child is not hurting or anxious. Watch what you say to or around them. Words matter and the words you say during this time will stick. Really think before you blurt something out that can do damage.

COWORKERS OR COLLEAGUES

Again, most people will display socially appropriate sympathy and empathy—that is, until it starts to affect them directly or they have judged that this has "gone on long enough." I don't have any amazing advice that will solve the problem. My best advice is to use your best judgment on how much time to take off and when. Don't forget about what you are permitted under the Family Emergency Medical Act. Not everyone can financially afford to take time off or as much as they would like. You just have to do your best. However, the impact and hard feelings will be lessened if, when you are at work, you are employing your best time-management skills as discussed in Chapter 4, and you are actually getting shit done.

It will be difficult for anyone to complain about you taking extra time off if you are getting your work product completed. If you are using the tools in Chapter 4, you will be getting more done, and better, than your coworkers, even if you are there half of the time they are. While they are gossiping with others and checking email and Facebook, you are producing. So, when you are at work, get it done. Then you can feel free to take more time off and leave work behind when you walk out the door.

Your brain can get fuzzy during this time. You are overloaded. So, if you can, have someone else check your final work product for accuracy. If that is not possible, then double- and triple-check your work and literally read it out loud. You will find mistakes that you have overlooked when you read it out loud. (You will thank me for this one.)

MEDICAL PERSONNEL

For the most part, I have only dealt with wonderful doctors, nurses, technicians, and social workers. Most are very skilled at answering your questions, being patient, and yet not giving false hope. Keep in mind that, although they know a lot, they still know less than they think they know. What I mean by this is that they are not fortune-tellers. They can't and won't give you definite answers that you so want.

It helps to ask them direct questions and follow-up questions. "So, when X happens, what then?" "What are the time parameters?" "What is the best possible scenario?"

My brothers and I had to make the decision to take my father off of the ventilator. As my aunt repeatedly said, it really wasn't our decision; his body was making the decision for us. Even though he had a very detailed living will and had been very clear in his instructions to myself and my brother that he didn't want to live in this condition, actually making the decision was still more difficult than I thought it would be. We had a family meeting with medical personnel, clergy, and social workers. Based on who was there, it was clear to me and one brother that they were signaling us that there was no hope and it was time to take him off the ventilator. Another brother was having a really difficult time understanding that our stronger-than-life father was not going to rally from this one. It was critical that he fully understood the reality or there would be a lifetime of "what ifs" and issues between us moving forward.

Even when I asked for best-case scenario, which was in an institution, maybe semiconscious for an hour a day and always on a ventilator or other breathing device, my brother wasn't getting it. Then he asked the magic question. He asked the doctor if my dad would be able to talk. His doctor said no, and my brother instantly got it. My dad lived to talk and if he couldn't talk, there was no point in living. You could see my brother do a 180 instantly.

At another point I had made a jackass comment about my dad traveling at Thanksgiving. My other brother took that to heart and began owning responsibility for my dad's condition. He started to question what if he had brought him in earlier to the hospital, not "let" him travel for Thanksgiving, yadda, yadda, yadda. Again, words matter, so watch what you say, and when in doubt, shut up. I had to make a special point of asking the doctor, in front of my brother, if there was anything anyone could have done to prevent this—knowing full well the answer was no.

When your parent is gone, you and your family will remain. It is okay to use the medical personnel to explain, comfort, and help make sure that there are not going to be residual "what ifs" after your parent dies.

Also recognize that, as close as you may get to medical personnel, especially the nurses, their job is to take care of your parent, not you. This sounds obvious until you are in the hospital day after day and forming relationships with the staff. I had an anxiety attack when my father was dying, as "his" nurse, who had cared for him each of the three times he was in ICU, had the audacity to think she was leaving at the end of her shift that evening. We were going to take him off the ventilator that evening. I totally freaked out that she would not be there when he died. I remember exclaiming "She can't; she said she would be here; she needs to stay; I will talk to her manager; she can get overtime..." total meltdown. Thank God my cousin was there and escorted me into the hall and calmed me down.

Of course, Cathy did leave that evening, as she should have, and the nurse who took her place was an angel, one of the most caring people I have ever met in my life. My point is, no matter how wonderful they are, they are not your friends. They will hug you and take great care of your loved one—they do not owe you anything but doing a great job.

OTHERS

It will be helpful to not have any preconceived notions or expectations of how other people will act during this time. People you barely know will go out of their way and do wonderful things for you, and people who are close to you will disappoint you. Hell, even when people specifically ask you what they can do to help you, and you tell them, don't expect them to do it or do it well. Seriously. Think about the person asking and if having them do something is going to actually add more stress if they won't do it well, on time, and so on. Only allow people to help you with vital things who you know will do it well and on time.

People also talk without thinking. What they say can be incredibly hurtful. You can't take it personally. It has nothing to do with you. It is all about them. You cannot pay attention to their hurtful words or carry them around with you. For instance, when I moved my mother from South Dakota to my home in Washington, evidently a lady, whom I had never met, made some ugly comment about why I would do that when I didn't even come to visit my mom. WTH? I had never met this woman. She had no idea when I came to visit, nor was it any of her business. Unfortunately, I carried that comment around with me for years. I continued to let her words affect me.

When my father was dying, a cousin, who was not there, questioned our decision to take him off of life support. I heard the comment through the other end of the phone and had an anxiety attack. Thank God my family was there and quickly calmed me down and centered me. My cousin had no flipping clue what she was talking about, wasn't there, had no say in the matter, and was talking out of fear and grief. She later called me, and we had a good conversation.

When I made the really stupid comment about what my dad shouldn't have done shortly before his last hospital trip, I was angry. I was just so angry that I was about to lose my dad. When I learned my baby brother was starting to blame himself for my dad's death, it stopped me in my tracks. I couldn't believe I had said such a stupid thing. I immediately took steps to rectify it and make sure that my brother knew that he had absolutely nothing to do with my dad's health or death and that I had made a stupid comment that wasn't even correct. However, the damage had already been done.

Please don't take what other people say to heart and really make sure that you hold your own tongue as well. How a family handles another family member's illness and death can either split a family forever or bring it closer together and form new relationships within the family.

Most of us have that one family member who is "the problem." In my family it is a cousin who I shall call Cora.

Cora has always caused turmoil, drama, and heartache for our family. My father would never completely shut her out, nor did he want us to do so. So we did what he wanted and invited her to come and say goodbye to him. We also knew that unless she was controlled, she would try to monopolize all time with him, to the exclusion of others, and maybe even cause a scene. She would try to get others to pay for her meals, hotel room, and so on. Hell, she tried to steal a ring off of my grandma's finger two hours after she died, so really nothing was off-limits to this woman.

Everyone at the hospital simply corralled her as much as possible. We informed the nurses who she was and what the rules were with her. We didn't leave her alone with my dad. At times, I told her that it was time to leave—once, three times. She still took liberties she had no business taking and made comments that she shouldn't have made, but it was tolerable. I also told myself that I was not going to let her interfere with my last day with my father. I was not going to get angry at her, as that was robbing me of my peace. Had I not made this conscious decision, I would have let her get to me.

When my father was dying, I made a conscious effort to make sure that all of my brothers knew what was going on and were included in decisions. Legally, my other brother and I didn't have to do that; however, morally we did, and if we wanted to keep our family together, which we sure as hell did.

Even if you are the leader in the family, don't abuse that power and influence. It is your job to care for other family members and be thoughtful of their feelings and your future as a family after this is over. When you snap, apologize. When you need some space, say so, and then take it. Lead, don't push.

What has been wonderful about my dad's death is that I have connected with family who I had not connected with before. I knew of them, talked on the phone to some, but had not met them. I should have met them years ago, but I let life get in the way. They are amazing people. I am so happy they are really in my life now. I regret it took my dad dying to connect with them, but so be it. I am not going to beat myself up anymore about that fact.

The bottom line is that there are some people who will go above and beyond to be wonderful to you during this time. Those are the people who have the emotional maturity and emotional intelligence to put your needs above their own during this time. That is probably about 20 percent of the population. The rest of them, when push comes to shove, put their own interests first. Don't expect any more from them.

For problem people, set clear boundaries in your head and, if needed, express those boundaries with those people, and most importantly, protect those boundaries. Communication is key. Say what you need. Say what you mean and mean what you say. Keep your own temper and words in check as well.

Above all else, remember that "this" will be over, but the rest of the people in your life will remain in some form or another. How you treat them, or how you react to their behavior and words, will make the difference between continuing a relationship with them or possibly severing it.

Chapter Nine

MONEY

///////////////

The only purpose of money in my life
is to buy time or comfort.
—TUCKER MAX

Money is such a tricky subject. We absolutely need it to live, much less live comfortably. Yet, cross that line and it is easy to obsess over it so much that it deprives you of both time and comfort.

I have always had a very complicated, and for the most part unhealthy, relationship with money. It is tempting to brush off any sort of in-depth discussion of money for another time, as there are far more "pressing" issues during this time of your life. However, whatever your money issues are, they will be magnified, as the process of dealing with a dying parent is incredibly stressful, and at times you are likely to hemorrhage money. At least get a little handle on your own money issues so that you can navigate this period in regard to money, as you are going to need to.

Unless your parent is independently wealthy, and by a freakin' lot, getting ill and dying in this country is ridiculously expensive, even if one is on Medicare and has supplemental insurance. Even supplemental insurance can cost over $800 per month. (I am not even going to go into the costs of medication or life-sustaining treatments.) Even if one is a millionaire, a few trips to intensive care can really hurt one's financial health. Long-term care insurance is increasingly difficult to even find, much less afford. In the future, it really isn't going to be an option. So that $15,000 per month care facility is likely going to be on your parents or you if not covered by Medicaid. If your parent has a disease that affects the brain, but not necessarily the body, such as Alzheimer's, they can live for years and need to live in a proper facility.

If you are facing a situation that is going to take long-term care, you should immediately talk to an elder law attorney (one who specializes in the same) about asset protection. There is only so much one can do, but saving something is better than losing everything.

So, the first step is to have some frank discussions with your parent(s) about the financial realities of their situation. How much money do they really have? You might be surprised. The first time my father was really ill I received a rather nasty surprise: his financial life was a big mess. He had, as many do, intertwined his personal and business finances and had some tax issues. I had to call in some favors from friends who were tax attorneys. It took a lot of work to sort it all out. He was embarrassed. The issue was resolved fairly easily, but it could have easily gone the other way, and during a difficult time the last thing you need is threats from the IRS.

In any case, you can't know how to proceed until you have an accurate picture of your parent's finances.

This may be a bit tricky in that your parent may resist this discussion or taking any action. It may be very difficult, understandably, for your parent to give up control of his or her finances or have someone else knowing about their finances. You know your parent. Tread lightly. The more you try to push and force the issue, the more your parent is going to resist, and ultimately, unless your parent is completely incapacitated, you have absolutely no say and no control.

The best way to approach it is to gently and kindly explain that at some point, either you or someone else is going to have to deal with your parent's finances. At that point, things will be far easier if some preparation is done beforehand. Bring in several financial advisors or elder law attorneys and have your parent choose one to work with. That way, there is more trust built. That is, of course, if they don't already have trusted counsel who has a proven track record of doing well for them.

The second step is to simplify the finances as much as humanly possible. I worked with one elderly couple who had over thirty-two accounts. It took me and the other attorney well over eighty hours apiece to sort out what accounts were active, what accounts had been transferred or closed, and so on. You don't want to have to hire a forensic accountant to figure out what is what. Is it really necessary for your parent to have a complicated portfolio? I don't know, but it is worth finding out. Do they have a bunch of investments that someone sold to them that are not really making them money? Now is the time to find out.

Work with a trusted financial planner—one who works for a fee, not commission. That way, you are paying for their advice, not paying for them to sell you crap. Get the accounts to a manageable number.

The third step is, with your parent's input and full consent, to formulate a plan on how to deal with the finances. Will there be enough money? Who is actually going to pay the bills? If there is not enough money, what bills get paid? Will property need to be sold in order to have more liquid?

COSIGNER ON ACCOUNT

I highly recommend that a trusted child be a cosigner on their parent's checking account. What this means is that both parties own the account and all funds in the account. It is critical that only a highly trusted other party be a cosigner. The benefit of being a cosigner is that you have full access to the funds at all times, before or after death. With this said, check with your estate attorney to ensure that you can have full access to the funds. In 2018, an appellate case came down in Texas which ruled that the cosigner on the account did not necessarily have full access to the deceased's funds.

I would not recommend having all of your parent's funds in the checking account, though. The only funds that should be in there are enough for a few months of bills. The point is to make paying bills easy, not to give you access to 100 percent of their funds. Not having all of the funds in a joint account will also give your parent some ease that they still control most of their funds. When the checking account is getting a bit low, they can transfer funds or write a check for another three months of bills, or whatever is appropriate. If something happens and they become incapacitated, you should still have enough in the checking account to cover you through the event or until you can legally access more funds.

FINANCIAL POWER OF ATTORNEY

Having an estate attorney or elder law attorney draft a financial power of attorney is also a good idea. This document allows you to legally handle your parent's financial affairs. It can be drafted to whatever specifications your parent wishes. For instance, it may say that you have the power to handle only certain accounts or transactions but not others, that you can sell stocks but not real property, or it can cover all financial powers. I highly recommend that two people are co-financial powers of attorney. This gives additional protection to your parent in that each person with the power of attorney knows that there is additional oversight. It also helps logistically in that the workload can be shared.

If you obtain a financial power of attorney, keep in mind that every penny is still your parent's money. You have a legal and moral fiduciary duty to care for their funds just like an attorney or bank. Every penny is for your parent's benefit—not yours. You don't get to pay yourself, throw other things in the grocery cart for yourself, or in any other way financially benefit because you have access to your parent's funds. So, again, your father's, mother's, grandparent's, whoever's money is for their time and comfort—not yours.

WHO MAKES THE DECISIONS?

This is a really easy question to answer. Your parent. As long as your parent can communicate to any reasonable degree, is lucid to any degree, then your parent gets to decide how to spend their money. Even if that means making bad decisions. Remember, it isn't your money, honey.

With that said, obviously keep an eye out for scams and other financial abusers. And have frank discussions with your parent about the same. To keep things simple, I would recommend having agreements beforehand, such as the agreement that as long as X bill doesn't exceed Y amount, you can just pay it. For instance, I was a cosigner on my mother's account. I paid her bills, bought her groceries, and so on. I knew her spending habits and never spent a penny more than she would. She had long-term care insurance, thank God. Her monthly bills were beginning to rapidly increase as we got closer to the end of life care.

So, if your parent is able, in any way, to make decisions, even really bad ones, they get to do that. If they are not, then use your best judgment, and do your best to do what your parent wants and would do themselves. However, when shit hits the fan, do what you need to do to keep them comfortable and well cared for.

WHO IS GOING TO PAY FOR ALL OF THIS?

If your parent(s) have their own money, insurance, Medicare, Medicaid, and so on, then all or most of their expenses should be paid by their funds. Things begin to get a bit trickier when they are not able to live independently, especially if they will be living with a child or other family member. If your parent is going to live with you, are they going to pay rent? Are you going to build a small apartment or other space for them? Who is going to pay for that?

It is important to have these conversations before the move so that everyone is on the same page. When we planned on having my father move into my home, I built a large room for him. We discussed that I would not charge him anything to live in my home. I would also cover basic groceries, utilities, and so on. However, he would need to pay for any extras like special food, medication, gas, entertainment, toiletries, and other basic costs. I knew what his monthly income would be, and his expenses would not exceed about 70 percent of his income from Social Security.

When my friend's grandmother was beginning to show signs that she could not live on her own, the original plan was for her to move in with her daughter, Samantha, my friend's aunt. Samantha was going to build onto her existing home to accommodate her mother. Then the question arose of who was going to pay for the addition, Samantha or Grandma? The addition was only for Grandma but would add to Samantha's home's value. Grandma also had the funds to pay for the addition. As it turned out, Grandma deteriorated quickly and had to move to an Alzheimer's home, so the issue was moot. However, the question remains for others.

Here is my suggestion to keep things "fair." The addition will add value to the property, but probably not enough to cover the costs. I think this comes down to your "why." Are you moving your parent in because they need to or to increase your property value? If it were me, and it was, I just made the extra space and didn't expect my dad to pay anything for it. If he had sufficient funds, then I am sure he would have insisted on paying "rent," and that would have helped with any additional costs. If you are keeping track of what you are spending to help your parent, then you are going to only cause grief for yourself. Decide what you can give and give it—or don't. But don't track it so that you can somehow try to recoup it later on or have some moral victory over other family members.

However, when your parent dies, if you are the personal representative, or are doing something specifically requested from the personal representative in connection with the estate, then do track your expenses for any estate-related costs, such as cremation, funeral, burial, or costs related to probate. The estate, if the estate has sufficient funds, should reimburse you for those. If the estate doesn't have the funds, then you are making a gift.

When my father died, I knew approximately how much money was in the estate. It wasn't much. My father never saved a penny in his life. I paid for his cremation, obituary, and memorial service. I knew that I would get some of the funds back, but probably not everything. My brothers didn't have the funds to really help out, so...I just did it. Maybe it wasn't fair, but life isn't fair. Be generous. If you can afford to do it, then just do it.

GET YOUR CHECKBOOK READY

Dying isn't cheap. Having a parent die isn't cheap. Not even going into the money value of your time, there are just a ton of extra expenses when shit really hits the fan, especially if you don't live within an hour of the hospital. There are last-minute flights that cost ten times the normal rate, rental cars, gas, Lyfts, hotels, eating out, family dinners eating out, heck, even new clothing if going to Montana or Chicago in December or January. You may also want to financially assist other family members who can't afford transportation to come see your parent.

When your parent dies, there are cremation or burial costs

that need to be paid right away. No, you won't be able to wait for life insurance proceeds before these bills get paid. They start at about $2,000 just for the cremation.

Then there are funeral costs, obituary costs, and attorney fees.

Depending on the circumstances, have at least $10,000 to $25,000 cash ready to go for these expenses. I am not kidding. I just had a client who paid over $17,000 for his wife's funeral. If your parent is aging and funds are tight, I recommend setting funds aside now so that you have at least a little wiggle room when things start to go down. The last thing you want is to not be able to make that flight or help someone else make that flight to say goodbye or attend a service.

No, none of your travel expenses, food expenses, and so on will be reimbursed from the estate. Those are on you, baby. On a side note, if your parent doesn't live close to you, investigate hotels/motels now, and pick a suitable one. When things start to go, they go very quickly. You don't have time to fully vet a suitable place to stay. You want to stay close to the hospital, at a hotel that is reasonably priced (probably) and of suitable quality. Quality is going to be important, as you are going to be stressed out enough and need some extra nurturing. The last thing you need after spending eight hours traveling, then another eight hours in the hospital is to come to a room that you don't feel comfortable in.

The first time my father got sick, I made a reservation at a motel that was within walking distance from the hospital. It was a national brand that was supposed to be midrange, especially for the small city he was in. The price was mid-range and the photos were acceptable. When we arrived, we were beyond exhausted, and it was 9:00 p.m. The first thing we saw was a drug deal in the parking lot. Then we saw people cooking dinner in their room. The room was ridiculous. Something out of a Quentin Tarantino movie. It was dirty and not well maintained, and the final straw was when my brother found a blood drop on the sheet. It was horrible. It still provides for great laughs at family get-togethers.

So, we moved to another motel, farther away from the hospital, that was much better, although it hadn't been decorated since 1972. At least it was clean, and I felt safe there. In hindsight, I would have insisted on just staying at a higher-end hotel. I would have been much more comfortable, and it would have been worth the extra $150 a night.

Again, in life, especially during this time, be generous. I am part of four separate family groups. Two of them have "those" people in them. The ones who never pay for anything, expect someone else to pay for every family meal, and so on. It can make me crazy. At times, I have gone to great lengths to not have to pay for their meal one more time. I don't mind giving, but I don't like people taking. During this time, however, I was far more generous and, as a result, far happier.

Helping other family members, who can't afford it, with a meal out or gas will make you feel amazing. Again, keep the "why" in mind. The family is there to support each other. Who the hell cares who paid for what? This is a temporary situation, and you don't ever need to pay for that cousin's meal again. Just have some class and suck it up.

If you really can't afford it, or "that" person has just taken one penny too much, then make sure that you communicate your expectations clearly, but nicely, before an event. For instance, if the family is all going to go eat, then tell the server, in front of everyone, that you all prefer separate checks. That way, everyone is on notice that they are on their own.

MONEY MANAGEMENT

If you do not have a history of healthy financial management, then perhaps you are not the best person to manage someone else's money. It is also a lot of work. So it might be in everyone's best interest to hire a bookkeeper, financial firm, or CPA to handle your parent's finances and pay bills. Yes, there will be a fee for this work, but it will be nominal and well worth the cost of not having to hassle with it. A professional firm will take on the liability of any mismanagement, not you.

If that is not financially available to you or you love handling the finances, then fine, go ahead. Just keep in mind, again, that you have a duty to put your parent's needs and interests first and foremost and to not take risks with their funds. Please talk to a reputable financial professional before doing anything other than paying bills. A professional can help you and your parent make difficult choices as well, such as how much liquid cash they really need versus investments. Whether to pay off debt or keep it around for a while. They should also know the basics of Medicare and Medicaid rules. However, if that is an issue, or may be in the future, then see an experienced estate planning attorney or elder law attorney to prepare for the possibility of these programs and possible asset protection.

IT AIN'T YOUR MONEY

Take a few minutes by yourself so that you can close your eyes and focus. Imagine men coming into your mother's home and taking away your grandma's hutch, your father's gun collection, or every penny they own. Whatever it is that you value the most of your parent's or other family member's things. Imagine a completely empty bank account when your father dies.

How does that feel? A little anxious? Do you have a knot in your stomach? My point is that you have to be at total peace with nothing being left of your parent's things at the end of the day. None of it is yours. What may or may not be yours in the future is none of your business. I don't care how long it has been in the family. I don't care how many times you have been told it would be yours someday. It isn't yours until it is.

I have touched on this before, but I saved this section for the last in this chapter because this is important. Only a small minority of people are thieves. Only a smaller percentage of thieves would steal from their own grandmother. Lots of people, however, think little of being able to justify giving themselves "advances" on "their" inheritance.

I have seen it too many times to count: from physically taking property "that is going to be mine anyway" before a person actually dies and the estate is settled, to "borrowing" money with no real intent on paying it back, to outlasting the older person, to actually taking funds from Grandma's purse. And then there is not spending on Grandma so she has money left to give me some.

I know it can be tempting to think about what you are going to inherit. I caught myself thinking about wearing my grandma's diamond ring before my mother actually died. It was at my home, as it was safer there than at the assisted living facility. However, it wasn't mine. It was still my mother's property.

People have literally killed their relatives to get their inheritance sooner than planned. There are actual laws that specifically state that you can't inherit if you killed the person in order to inherit. It is tempting to plan ahead on what you can do with "the money" or where you will put that priceless family treasure. *Don't go there.* Just don't go there.

Getting any inheritance is no different than getting a birthday gift. If you happen to get something, then great. If not, fine. You have absolutely no right to receive a thing. No one owes you anything. Your parent's property is his or her property. He can do whatever he wants with it. Now, of course, most people, probably your parents included, want their family to receive family heirlooms. They might also want to pass down money to help future generations. None of that is relevant to the fact that you cannot have the mindset that it is yours until a judge or trust administrator says it is yours.

So, the two most important things to remember about

money are that if you are handling someone else's money, you have a fiduciary duty to that person, just like a bank, and you had better not fuck it up. Also, it ain't your money. Repeat after me: "It isn't my money. I am owed nothing."

If you do happen to inherit anything, be flippin' grateful. One doesn't receive a handmade jar of jam for their birthday and bitch because they didn't get the entire jam company for their birthday. Same goes with inheritance. Whatever you receive, whether it be a dime or $1 billion, is a gift. Treat it as such.

Chapter Ten

ESTATE PLANNING

///////////////////////

Before death takes away what you have been
given, give away what there is to give.
—RUMI

I am an estate planning attorney so, yes, there will be a chapter in this book on estate planning. Don't worry; it isn't depressing or morbid. If you think of it in a different light, it can actually be fun.

When you die, not if, you will either leave a legacy for others or a mess for someone (probably someone you love) to clean up. Those are your two options. The only two options. You can either give people you love a gift of an easy transition, or a mess of wasted time, wasted money, fighting amongst themselves, resentment, and the last memory of you to be that you left them a fucking mess. Sometimes a literal mess.

Likewise, your parent is either going to leave a legacy or a mess. You may very well be the person who has to clean up the mess if one is left. Therefore, encouraging your parent to ensure that his or her affairs are in order with proper estate planning is going to be important. One of the best gifts your parent can give you is getting their estate plan done.

What is estate planning? Simply put, estate planning is the legal process of carrying out your wishes if you are unable to communicate, taking care of your finances, and what we do with you and your property and debt when you die. If you don't do your own estate plan, the "state's" estate plan will be used and that is probably different than what you, or your parent, would like.

Yet many people don't spend the time or money to get their estate plan done properly. I get many inquiries. Many "I know I need to do this" comments. But the majority of people are not willing to face the stark reality that...You are going to die. There is no bargaining out of this fact. You can ignore it, but that won't affect the outcome. There is a deep biological desire to live in every cell in every one of us. Our brain's and body's only function is to keep us alive. So, while, logically, we know that we are going to die, that fact goes against everything our brain and body are trying to do every day. Hence the resistance to anything to do with death.

It takes a conscious decision to put on your grown-up pants and do what you need to do to get your estate plan in order. You can cheat and say you did it, when all you did was go online or work with a subpar attorney, but as in everything else, there are no shortcuts to anything of value.

Your choices, and your parent's choices, are that you can ignore reality and do nothing, you can do cheap and easy, or you can dig deep, grow up, and make the investment of time and money necessary in order to leave a legacy. Both for your parents and for yourself.

THE HELL THAT IS LEFT WITHOUT PROPER PLANNING

The stories are simply too numerous, as they happen literally every single day. I would guess that you have some of your own about friends and family members.

Proper planning is the difference between things going as one wants at the end of life versus having hiccups, bills not paid, and being kept alive when you don't want to be. It is the difference between a family staying together and splitting apart after a parent dies. The difference between money being used to help people versus being used to destroy a person unequipped to handle it.

Improper planning, or no planning, leads to people

coming out of the woodwork to claim parentage and money when you die without any estate plan, as the artist Prince did. Or the drug-addicted nineteen-year-old daughter getting a check for $150,000 when her father died. Or one's adult children not being able to have access to you, because your second wife has literally taken you from your assisted living facility, in the dead of night, as Casey Kasem's wife did. It took court orders for his children to see him. Finally, he was placed in their care, as there were more than a few questions about his wife's care of him. When he died, his wife took his body and wouldn't tell his children where it was. Not kidding.

While these stories may make the news, others just like them happen every day. Proper estate planning matters. In your own family, what possible messes would occur if your parent, or you, were to become incapacitated or die without proper planning?

WHAT IS PROPER ESTATE PLANNING?

Proper estate planning is simple, but not cheap. It is going to an attorney, who frankly only does estate planning or maybe estate planning and elder law, who has years of experience, and who values their work product. You should expect to make a financial and time investment. Probably far more than you expect. When you go cheap, what you are getting is an old template that may or may not be current to the law and that either doesn't give you the available options or you have no idea what options are best.

Even if one doesn't have much money, it is vital to spend the money and do things properly. Why? Because you do it and think it is done properly, and then find out, or your family finds out, that it wasn't and you can't fix it. You have a false sense of security that you are covered when you are not.

So please do what you can, while respecting boundaries, to get your parent to spend the money and get their estate plan done properly. You will save your family untold money and, more importantly, anxiety and heartache.

ESTATE PLANNING BASICS

Below is a highly simplified conversation about estate planning. It is not meant to be a primer in the law. Each state's laws are different. Talk to a good estate planning lawyer and have her answer any questions. For God's sake, don't take anything below as legal advice. I don't know your facts, you are not my client, and I don't practice in forty-eight of the fifty states in the United States.

Power of Attorney (Financial)

A power of attorney (financial) is a legal document that

grants all of the power to an individual to control another adult's finances. It can be generic or highly specific. For instance, it can grant only certain powers in regard to finances but not others, such as buying or selling property. It can have effective dates or events included as well.

So, if I have your financial power of attorney, I can access your bank accounts (in theory) and other financial accounts. I can pay your bills, take out debt in your name, sell your property, or buy property in your name. Depending on the language, I can do everything you could do with your money.

One wants to be very careful with granting anyone else a power of attorney, as that person can literally take all of your money and property. You are giving 100 percent control to that other person, unless specified otherwise. For instance, I knew someone who gave his wife a power of attorney in regard to the purchase of a home. She told him it would simplify things, as he wouldn't have to sign any of the documents. In reality, she had run up tens of thousands of dollars of credit card debt and didn't want him to find out through the mortgage process. So along with a brand-new mortgage, he also got tens of thousands of dollars in credit card debt that he had not been aware of.

Again, don't forget that if you have someone's power of

attorney, you have a fiduciary duty to them and to do right by them. Otherwise, you are just a thief. Do we need to review the last chapter?

Medical Power of Attorney

A medical power of attorney is a legal document that gives another adult legal authority to make medical decisions on your behalf. Regardless of whether one has a medical directive or not, there are a thousand and one medical decisions that need to be made that will not be covered by the medical directive. This is just the nature of the beast, as any medical issue, much less end of life, is very fluid.

Whoever has the medical power of attorney should be someone who is emotionally strong enough to make the hard calls and not bow down to pressure from other family members who may not agree. I highly recommend that that person also be physically close, as it is one thing to talk to a doctor over the phone and an entirely different thing to actually see, hear, and feel what is happening to your parent.

Whom you choose to give your medical power of attorney to is up to you. It doesn't have to be a family member. Most people have their spouse or children as their medical power of attorney. Some have friends. Whomever you trust to be able to advocate for you, who has a level head, and will do "right" by you is who you want.

If you are not chosen to hold your parent's medical power of attorney, don't take it personally. It is not about you.

Medical Directive (Living Will)

A medical directive, sometimes called a living will, is a legal document in which you give medical personnel instruction on what extraordinary medical treatments you want, or do not want, in the event you are not able to communicate. A medical directive only goes into effect if you are really not able to communicate. So even if you can respond appropriately to questions by squeezing a hand, pointing, and so on, then you will be able to make your own medical decisions.

Most people in the medical field have seen some pretty horrible consequences of trying to keep people alive, or actually keeping them alive, past their natural expiration point. Keeping someone alive artificially isn't pretty and comes at some fairly high costs, financial being the least dramatic. Most of my clients, and people I know, want medical personnel to try to "save" them, but only if their quality of life will be acceptable.

Some people want the whole menu. My grandfather

Wolden wanted anything that could be done to keep him alive. That is fairly unusual. Most people want extraordinary care if it will be for a short duration or there is a real chance that they will regain brain function.

For instance, my father was fine with one to three dialysis treatments but didn't want to be on dialysis for any length of time.

If there is one gift you and your parent can give to your family, it is to be very clear about what you do and don't want. Answer the question "If I can't do X, Y, or Z, then I don't want to keep going." I can tell you, as someone who has had to make the decision to turn off life-sustaining procedures, it is one of the most difficult things I have ever had to do. There was absolutely no question he would not have wanted to go on, and yet it was excruciatingly difficult, and it was still easy to start second-guessing myself with "what ifs."

Please don't do that to your family. Don't let your parents do that to you.

This document is critical. In any event, make your wishes known, in writing, so that your family has emotional "permission" to do what needs to be done.

HIPAA Release

With the advent of HIPAA, one needs to have a HIPAA release, which is a legal document that tells medical staff whom they can share your medical information with and whom they can't. Most people are okay with their family having their medical information. However, many people have an estranged parent, child, or sibling with whom they don't want their personal information shared.

Make it simple and your wishes clear on who can get medical information and if there is anyone specifically who shouldn't get it. Keep in mind that the hospital personnel have other things going on. They are not going to do a background check on someone when that person calls and says they are your mother. So, if your biological mother or someone else is not someone who should get your information, it is up to you to make that clear.

Will

We all know what a will is, right? It is a legal document that indicates how a person wants his or her estate (money and property) to be divided and distributed when he or she dies. And no, writing something on a napkin won't work. There are extremely strict requirements that vary state to state on what a legal will needs to include. Again, I would strongly, like hit you over the head strongly, advise that you need a specialized attorney to do this correctly.

Keep in mind that legally (in every state I have checked), regardless of what a will may or may not say, if you have any money, your final expenses (funeral, legal fees, cremation, and so on) are to be paid first, then last hospital bills, and then your creditors. Only if something is left can it be distributed to heirs.

Trust

Trusts are amazing. Before I started practicing estate planning, I thought, like many other people, that trusts were this thing out in space, only for rich people. *Not* true. It might be very possible that your parent needs a trust, or you do, and therefore, I will give a small description of the benefits of trusts.

The legal trust is a legal instrument in which one person's property is held for the benefit of a person. That means nothing, right? So here is how I explain it to my clients, even highly financially sophisticated clients.

A trust is like an empty bucket. We fill the bucket with property. We can put your house, your money, your businesses, or anything else in the bucket. If we have a revocable (can get rid of the trust) living trust (RLT), then you own the trust. So, you still own everything in the bucket. You can take things out of the bucket and put more things into the bucket. When we put property into the bucket this is called "funding." So, if you haven't actually put the property into the bucket, the trust is not funded, and you have an empty bucket. Which is worthless.

So, while you are alive and not incapacitated, having a trust really doesn't affect your life much, if at all. The magic of a trust happens when you are either incapacitated or die. If you are incapacitated, then the property in the trust will be used as you have directed for your benefit or others' benefit. When you die, the property in the trust will be used and distributed for the people you have designated (beneficiaries) in the way you want. Sounds like a will, right?

Here is the magic of the trust that totally differs from a will.

1. Probate. If you have a fully funded trust when you die, your estate will not have to go through probate. Your trust can be administered in an attorney's office. Probate is really expensive, and the estate will be paying for it. Generally, 4 to 8 percent of the estate. That can add up to tens of thousands, if not hundreds of thousands of dollars. Yes, you will have to pay attorney fees and other costs for the trust to be administered, but nothing compared to probate.

    Probate is time-consuming. Even when states have

enacted "easy" probate procedures, it still takes a lot of time and is a hell of a lot of work. I had one friend who was a financial planner, so she knew her stuff, and she kept track of the hours she spent administering her father's estate through probate. Even with an attorney, she spent over 450 hours. Do you have 450 hours to spend on this project?

Probate is totally public. So, anyone can learn about what you have and who is getting it. This leads to lots of issues with identity theft and predators targeting beneficiaries, especially the young and elderly. Do you really want anyone to be able to learn, immediately, that your nineteen-year-old son just inherited $250,000? Probably not.

2. Asset protection. Asset protection is the main reason most people have an RLT. There are other types of trusts, but we are not going to discuss them here. The items of property that are in the trust are protected for their beneficiaries against creditors, predators, and self-defeating behavior, if written into the trust. This can get complicated, and this chapter is not meant to be a primer in trusts. So, again, talk with your estate attorney.

Trusts can also make specific distributions for whatever purpose you would like and whatever conditions you would like, such as the trust paying for college, a down payment on a first house, or anything else that you might feel is important to help the beneficiary with.

3. Using your money to help people, not harm them. Many of us have had the dubious pleasure of meeting the "trust fund kid," and what sticks with us is that that kid is emotionally immature, self-centered, lazy, materialistic, and a total jerk. Trust me, over-giving to anyone to the point where they don't have to do anything to have a "great lifestyle" is not doing them any favors. When someone has unlimited access to seemingly unlimited money, without any expectations, nothing good generally comes from it.

My clients want their funds to help the people they love, not harm them. So, we always include lifestyle and health provisions in our trust. In short, they say that if the trustee suspects that a beneficiary is using drugs, abusing alcohol, or has some other issue that is self-destructive that the trustee can stop distributions. This is of course with conditions to protect the beneficiary.

So, in summary, if done properly and with thought, a trust is an amazing vehicle to be able to preserve one's assets, maybe for future generations, save money, and to really help the people you love. The best part is they are not just for the rich. Anyone who would avoid probate (assets over $100,000 in some states) could benefit from a trust. So, at the very least, talk to an experienced estate attorney who has experience with trusts.

If you are the one who is going to be dealing with your parent's estate, it is going to be even more important that their estate is done properly so that you don't have unnecessary work or stress.

WHO IS GOING TO DO ALL OF THIS?

Your personal representative and/or trustee, or your parent's, should be someone who is sophisticated enough to be able to handle the rigors of the job, which is quite a bit, even with the assistance of an attorney. They need to be strong enough to withstand any pressure from beneficiaries as well. No, they won't need a PhD, just common sense and a strong backbone. Needless to say, it should be someone you trust.

It should also be someone who is not going to put their interests first or have power issues with the beneficiaries. For instance, I knew a woman who went power-happy when she was the personal representative of her father's estate. Anyone who knew her knew that she was the last person who should be in charge, as she would abuse her power. Her actions split the family in two. Don't pick that person. If the person has a history of not being able to get along with people, has a chip on his or her shoulder, or is just a jerk, don't pick that person.

So, whom you should choose for all of this is up to you, with the advice of your estate planning attorney. A good attorney is going to ask you about whom you are choosing and why, to ensure the right fit. Put some thought into whom you are choosing, though, as it really is important. Also, you will need alternatives in case your first choice isn't willing or able to do the job.

CONVERSATIONS AND COPIES

Once your parent's, or your, estate plan is done, keep the originals in a "safe" place. This *does not* include a safety deposit box, as when you die, no one can get into it quickly or without a court order. Make sure that everyone who has a job in your estate plan has a copy of documents that pertain to him or her. Additionally, the people with your power of attorney should know and have easy access to the originals. That is because a bank may (their own policy) require the original to be brought in before they give access to an account.

Also, when you have your estate plan drafted, or while drafting it, you may want to discuss your plans with your beneficiaries. Not that they get a vote, but you never know what may be really important to one person that you might want to include in your plan. It also might be helpful to avoid any future tension if everyone is clear on your plan and your wishes. That way, there can't be any argument that Mom really wanted X or that Sister convinced Mom to do Y. With a family conversation, there is absolutely no doubt as to what is going to happen.

COMPETENCY

I am not going to say a lot on this subject other than that there is a very long distance between when a person is fully competent and when that person is clearly unable to handle their own affairs and decisions. People are embarrassed at memory lapses and go to great lengths to hide the same. People might not realize themselves that something is "off." It is difficult to tell whether Dad's "offness" or lapse in memory is just him getting older, perhaps a drug he is on, or if something is really wrong. Even when it is clear that there is a memory issue, that still doesn't mean that the person is not able to handle his affairs, much less make life decisions.

When you begin to notice things that are strange with your parent or start saying, "I told you that" more and more, start to keep a log. Talk to his or her doctor. Maybe offer a bit more help, but don't push unless absolutely necessary for safety. You are going to create a firestorm if you try to tell your parent that you are taking over because they are incompetent. That is, even if they know that they are having some memory issues.

If your parent is refusing to accept help, and there is a safety issue, then you really need to speak with a great elder law attorney. Just know that the bar to finding someone incompetent is extremely high, for very good reason.

In order to execute an estate plan, your parent will need to be able to understand that he or she is executing a will or other estate document; know what property they own; without prompting, know who their heirs are; and know the general contents and important specific provisions of the documents.

ADMINISTRATION

Whether there is a will, no will, or a trust, your parent's estate will need to be administered in some fashion. I cannot emphasize enough that this is a big task, takes a long time, and must be done correctly. If you are the personal representative, administrator, or trustee, it is imperative that you hire competent counsel to assist you. Yes, even a simple estate is a pain in the ass to take care of. It is going to take more time and energy than you think. It is imperative that you fully understand your responsibilities, as you have personal liability if you screw up. So, hire a good estate attorney, understand your duties, and jump in and get it done.

CONCLUSION

One of the best gifts your parents can ever give you and the rest of the family, bar none, is doing their estate plan and doing it properly. You also have a responsibility, as a full-grown adult, to the other people in your life to get your own estate plan done as well. You never know; you could die before your parents. Their great estate plan will not work if you don't have one in place too.

So, like anything else in life do it, do it well, as there are no short cuts, and make the investment. Leave a legacy, not a mess.

Chapter Eleven

AFTER DEATH

No one ever told me that grief felt so like fear.
—C.S. LEWIS

"Okay, Mom, I have slept; you can come back now." These were my exact thoughts after getting two full nights of sleep after my mom died. Depending on the circumstances, you will probably have some adrenaline rush around the time your parent dies, even if their death is unexpected or sudden. When that adrenaline wears off, wow, talk about exhaustion. Do not underestimate the toll managing a parent's death takes on your body, emotions, mind, and spirit. You are going to be freaking tired—exhausted. You may have trouble sleeping, but you also may sleep nine hours a night and still need a good nap the next day. This may go on for a few days, weeks, or months. If at all possible, take the time your body needs to rest. Even if you think it is "too much," for now, just sleep. If it goes on for more than a month or two, then maybe talk to your doctor to make sure you are not sleeping due to depression.

One other thing to immediately talk about, after sleep, is that it is okay for you to feel relief after your parent dies. I am going to say this again as it is that critical for you to absorb. *It is okay for you to feel relief when your parent dies.* You are not a bad person. It doesn't mean you didn't love your parent or think you are better off because he is dead. Unless your parent wasn't good for you. Then maybe you are better off.

What it means is that this was a bad situation. It might have been a long, drawn-out illness in which you saw your parent in pain, miserable, depressed, and not herself. There might have been years of addiction, which is miserable. Your life has been turned upside down. It is totally normal for you to have some relief that "this" is over and that your life is going to get back to "normal." (Well, a new "normal," as it is never going to be the same.) It is okay to realize that, while you want your parent to live "forever," it is as he or she was, healthy, happy, vibrant, and able to do things. Not like "this."

Again, maybe you also had a really crappy parent. You are not alone. If your parent brought you a lot of pain during your life, it is only natural for you to feel relief when that pain is gone. You might also feel grief for what should have been. The parent they should have been to you. The world is not always better because certain people are in it. It is okay to acknowledge that and feel relief. Really.

THE FIRST WEEK

Besides sleeping, there is a lot that needs to be done, and done quickly, after your parent dies. First is, of course, to notify other family members. Instead of calling everyone yourself, designate another family member, if possible, to enact a phone tree to notify people so that it is not all on your shoulders. If your parent is employed, then their employer will need to be notified as well.

The first day, you will need to make arrangements for the body, whether it be cremation, burial, or some other arrangement. Generally, the hospital or hospice can help you pick a funeral home, and they will pick up the body. You will need to go to the funeral home and inform them as to cremation, burial, or any other alternative. Be prepared to pay them immediately. This can range from $2,000 for a basic cremation to $20,000-plus for a full burial and funeral. That doesn't include food or car service. Liquid cash on hand is going to be important.

If you have chosen cremation, then you have some time to plan any service. You can relax a bit. If the body will be buried, then unfortunately, you are going to have to get moving and plan the funeral within a week or so. I think that is really tough emotionally to do so quickly, but that is up to your parent's wishes.

If the body is cremated, you have some time to plan a service, but others still want to know fairly quickly if it is going to be immediate or if they have some time to plan. So, have some general idea of the timing of the service. Even if you are "in charge" of making arrangements, make sure to include other important individuals, such as siblings, in the decision making. Now is not the time for any power issues to come to the surface. She was their mom just as much as yours. This time is critical and can pull a family together or split it apart—depending on whether people are treated with kindness and respect or not.

The funeral director, even if you are not having a funeral, will be helpful to you in some of the other tasks that should be done within the first week. Most will give you some brochures with great checklists on what to do. I am not going to go into detail here, but they include notifying employers, banks, investment services, and so on. The funeral home should notify Social Security, so you don't need to worry about that. They will also order death certificates for you. I recommend getting ten copies, just to be safe, as most institutions want them to be certified. Also notify your parent's estate attorney so that she is ready to advise the personal representative and get things moving legally.

Take some time for self-care that first week. Whether it is getting a few long massages, going for good walks in the park or woods, or whatever else is your soul food. You are also probably going to be spending some time that first week with family. Again, this can be a great time to heal, get to know one another, and come together as a family, if handled well. Remember, other people are hurting too.

Recognize that your mind is going to be really fuzzy, almost like you were drunk or on drugs. Your brain is totally overloaded, and even simple thinking tasks may be difficult. Be kind to yourself and others who are grieving. Don't try to do difficult mental tasks right now, even balancing your checkbook. You are going to drop balls and make mistakes. So try to keep the thinking tasks pretty simple right now.

THE FIRST MONTH

The first month, you are probably getting back to your life. You are working again, taking care of your own family, and life is moving on. The adrenaline is gone. The phone calls and check-ins probably have stopped. Now is when you really get to either deal with your feelings or ignore them. I would highly suggest not ignoring them. You should be still practicing your self-care so that you can complete the tasks that need to be completed.

The personal representative should meet with the estate attorney within the first month to see what needs to be done and get started. If you are the personal representative, know that there are legal time frames that need to be met. You don't get to stall or not deal with your duties until you "are ready."

During this first month, you should have a good idea of the dates and type of service, if any, you are planning and have that fairly planned out and communicated with people. Publishing an obituary is also customary. You may have even started going through your parent's things. Don't do this without speaking with the estate attorney first, though. Nothing gets other family members' hackles up so fast as one family member starting to grab stuff. Even if you are authorized to get rid of stuff, be thoughtful to other members of your family. Even if they are not a beneficiary of any estate plan, they might like a personal object or two.

When my uncle died, my cousins, Greg and Hal, had limited time and just started working on getting rid of stuff at the house quickly. They were both busy and focused on getting the house cleaned out. By the time I arrived four days later, the house had been cleaned out. They assumed no one would want the old household stuff and only saved "the good stuff." Well, I had no interest in the "good stuff." What I wanted were the two 1970s avocado green, ugly as sin flour and sugar containers that my Aunt Lou and I always got out when we baked together. They were already at the dump by the time I arrived. So, just as a thoughtful gesture, before you start throwing out stuff, ask family if anyone wants to go through and see if they want something sentimental.

THE SECOND MONTH AND BEYOND

You should have some handle on any legal responsibilities, the service is probably taken care of or well planned, and you can start to relax a bit. You won't get the same support anymore from other people. The "my dad just died" is over, and people expect you to get back on your feet and be normal. No one is calling to check in on you anymore or sending you cards. Yet you may still feel just as heart-broken as you did a month ago. Grief is a funny thing, and everyone handles it differently. I generally find it comes in waves and at inopportune times. At times I still cry over my mom, and she died well over a decade ago.

I am a total crier; my son Nathan is not. To my knowledge, he has never cried about either of his grandparents dying, and he was extremely close to my mother and close to my father. He may have cried in private, but he certainly has never teared up in public. My youngest brother, Andrew, also is not a crier. This really worried me when our father died. I even told him that I was going to start punching him until he started to cry. He is my little brother—I still get to punch him. I, along with others, was worried that he just wasn't dealing with my father's death, but he was, just in his own way. Once I recognized that he was grieving in his own way, and privately, I felt much better.

SIX MONTHS

Within the first six months, the estate process should be going, any service done, and your life fairly back to your new "normal." If you are still having such grief that it is affecting your life, I would highly recommend seeing a grief counselor.

I recommend that you take a vacation. A relaxing, nour-ishing vacation, not one to Disneyland or someplace where you want to see ten things a day. A do-nothing-but-look-at-sand-for-five-hours-a-day vacation. Or maybe five days at a spa. One where you feel fully rested, relaxed, and ready to come home and hit the ground running.

I made many mistakes when my mother died. Perhaps my biggest mistake was that I had planned on going to a spa for five days and then driving around Arizona for another few days after she died. The little bit of money

I would inherit would have more than taken care of this trip, and God did I need it. After my mom died and I completed her small and easy estate, I thought it was best to use the little money to pay off debt rather than "splurge" on myself. *Huge* mistake. My body and soul needed this rest and nourishment. It was going to get it one way or another. So I started coming into the office late, leaving early, or not coming in at all. At the end of the day, I took far more time off than I would have by going on vacation, and I never felt nourished, rested, or ready to go back to work fully. Spending $5,000 on myself would have been the best investment I could have made. Lesson learned.

After things have really settled down, take some time and reflect on what it is that you learned from this experience and what you want to take away in your life from your parents. How do you want to honor them by the way you live now? This can be hard in that no parent is perfect and some are really shitty. You learned something, though, even from the shitty ones. So how can you make your life better going forward because your parent was your parent?

Now is also the time to deal with, maybe with a professional, any lingering feelings of resentment or unresolved issues toward your parent. They aren't going to go away on their own, and they have and will continue to affect your life now, whether you recognize or acknowledge it or not.

UNRESOLVED ISSUES

My dad didn't do deep talks. He was the toughest, strongest person I have ever known. Think tough cowboys times ten. But he said "I love you" to me every single day. It wasn't until he died though that I really knew what I meant to him. It was through the words of other people that I learned just how proud of me he was and that I had changed his life when I found him. I learned from an uncle that my dad really felt he missed out on not knowing me until I found him at twenty-three. I had suspected some of his "discipline" of me, as a full-grown adult, was an attempt to make up for lost time, but now it was confirmed. I still tear up thinking about that. Others said that when he met me, my dad softened, which is frankly difficult to believe. I was his "little girl." Talk about healing.

With my mother, we had a more complex relationship. She had her own significant issues that prevented her from fully engaging with me emotionally and caused her to fail to protect me in a really significant way. I had been to therapy and had done a lot of work. I had fully recognized that my mom's reaction was her own issue and not mine. I had always wished, however, that she had owned what happened and her role in it. She never did, even on her deathbed.

I had always suspected, for various reasons, that my mother had been sexually abused. Only a few years ago, my fear was confirmed that my mother had been molested by her father. When I learned this, pure rage instantly filled me like I had never felt before. I got so protective of my mother and had my grandfather been alive, I would have done him real harm. For the first time, I could sense my mother's sorrow and full acknowledgment that she had failed me, just as she had been failed. Any resentment or negative feelings toward my mom instantly disappeared. I ended up ripping up a few photographs of my grandfather and then burning them. It felt like he finally had been confronted with what he had done. Even though he had been dead for forty-five years, his secret was out. I knew.

I don't know what happens after we die. I do know that both of my parents have gotten into my head since they died, and my conversations with each are as real as me sitting here typing. It has been absolutely wonderful knowing that there is still some connection there with each of them. It doesn't mean that my heart still doesn't ache.

YOUR TAKEAWAY

Your final step, final to do, in this process, is to take some time and reflect on how you want things to go down when it is your time. Yes, it will be your turn someday. If you have not done so yet, get your damn estate plan in proper order. But also talk to your family about what you have learned, what you would do differently, and how you want them to handle things when it is your turn. This might be scary to think about doing, but once you start the conversation, it is really pretty easy, and you will feel so much better afterwards. I remember when my dad was doing his estate plan, he said a few times, "no fighting." My brothers and I didn't ever fight with each other, but I assured him "no fighting." We kept that promise and remembered it during some emotional times. "No fighting." Thanks, Dad.

CONCLUSION

I wanted to include a story about someone who had done this perfectly. I couldn't find that person because she doesn't exist. You will make mistakes. You will fail. Know that going in. But not all of the time. There will be times when you might lose your shit, but with the tools in this book, those times will be fewer and less extreme.

I hope that, at this point, you fully realize that this is a big-ass deal and you need to treat it as such and be kind to yourself and others. If you are not treating it like a big deal, then you are likely in denial or minimizing the impact, and that will come back to bite you. So, now you are ready to face reality, put on your big-kid panties, and do what needs to be done for yourself and your parents.

Even if you drop a ball or two, you are not doing it wrong. As prepared as you are, and will continue to be, there is really no way you can ever be totally prepared to handle this situation and the emotions that come with it. Just do your best.

Learning without executing what you have learned is useless. Actually, it is worse than useless, as you know you know better, and when you fail to execute what you know, you betray yourself and feel like crap. I wrote this book for you. Both of my parents are dead, and writing a book is ridiculously difficult. This book is not to motivate you but to get you to modify your behavior so that this process is as good as it can possibly be. You may even grow and heal during this time.

If you really incorporate the tools provided in this book into your life, not only will it make this journey much easier, but it can actually improve the rest of your life. How much better will your life be when you can get the really important things done every single day and still have time left over? How great will your life be when you can have healthy boundaries with people and not be taken advantage of or taken for granted? How great will you feel knowing that if you do have to handle your parent's estate that it will be as simple and easy as possible, and any funds will be used to help people? Imagine how much of an adult you will feel like when you have your own estate plan wrapped up with a beautiful bow on it. What relief you will feel knowing that you are doing what you can so that when your time comes to be taken care of, you have set an amazing example.

So, breathe, do the work in each chapter, and know that

you are the exception and did your absolute best to do right by your parent.

One of my core values, and what motivates me, is to make an impact in the world. I might never change the world, but I can help one person at a time and make a difference in that one person's life. Obviously, the more people I help, the bigger the impact I can make. So, part of this journey is to ask for help when I need it. I am asking for *you* to help me make an impact. Please send me a testimonial of how this book was useful to you or how it can be improved. I want your emails or letters. Then, and only then, will I know I am reaching my goals and making an impact. Also, when you know of someone else who is likely to, or is actually taking care of their parent, send them a copy of this book.

Thank you for honoring me with your most precious resource: your time. I look forward to hearing from you.

Brita Long

One life on this earth is all that we get, whether it is enough or not enough, and the obvious conclusion would seem to be that at the very least we are fools if we do not live it as fully and bravely and beautifully as we can.
—FREDERICK BUECHNER

ABOUT
BRITA LONG

BRITA LONG is an estate planning attorney, writer, and speaker. She has been a mother, stepmother, daughter, sister, wife, ex-wife, business owner, and amateur trapeze artist, has wing-walked over the Salish Sea, and has saved two old homes from certain death. She lives in Austin, Texas, with her dog, Bear. *Soon She Will Be Dead: A Comprehensive Guide to Losing Your Parent without Losing Your Mind* is her first book. Learn more at BritaLong.com.